Henry Jennings

Heavenly Melodies

Being Original and Selected Poems

Henry Jennings

Heavenly Melodies
Being Original and Selected Poems

ISBN/EAN: 9783337006174

Printed in Europe, USA, Canada, Australia, Japan

Cover: Foto ©Thomas Meinert / pixelio.de

More available books at **www.hansebooks.com**

Heavenly Melodies;

BEING

ORIGINAL AND SELECTED POEMS.

BY

HENRY JENNINGS.

DEDICATED, BY SPECIAL PERMISSION, TO

SIR ELKANAH ARMITAGE, KNT.

TO BE HAD OF

THE AUTHOR, TADLEY, NEAR BASINGSTOKE.

MDCCCLXIV.

This Volume

IS,

BY SPECIAL PERMISSION,

MOST RESPECTFULLY DEDICATED TO

SIR ELKANAH ARMITAGE, Knt.,

BY HIS HUMBLE AND DEVOTED SERVANT

HENRY JENNINGS.

Preface.

It is necessary that I should state very briefly the design of this volume, which is sent forth with some degree of diffidence.

Its object is to interest, and, with the Divine blessing, to benefit precious immortal souls. I have made choice selections from the works of the most eminent and godly men of various denominations of Christians—from the writings of men who were in doctrine and practice sound and correct; who were immoveably firm, like those stones which an infant's finger can touch, but no giant's arm can throw; who were one in heart with every Christian, regardless of minor differences and sectarian distinctions; whose spirits were so lofty, pure, and aspiring, that they seemed to be seraphs confined in a tenement of clay; whose zeal, which burned without consuming them, arose from a vehement desire to serve God, apart from every other consideration than the glory, excellence, and holiness of the Divine character; whose lives harmonized with their profession; whose sentiments accorded with Divine revelation: whose love for souls was paramount to all personal influence of any kind, even of the particular sections of Christians with whom they were identified; whose unity with every believer in Jesus as to the essentials of Christianity and the fundamental principles of the glorious Gospel of the blessed God was complete and cordial; whose force of thought, strength of feeling, power of imagination, ardour of eloquence, and energy of language constituted them poets of the first order, and secured them world-wide fame.

Some sentences are gems of inestimable value; some pieces sparkle with the light of immortality; others glow with a deep, mild,

autumnal lustre, as if reflected from the face of Him who dwells in
the excellence of His Father's glory. Some rise into rich rhetoric
from intricate and laborious argument ; others are simple as the
beatings of the purest and most loving heart. All are true, all are
good : they are the breathings of souls moved by the Holy Ghost.
Some lines admonish the ungodly—they warn them to flee from the
wrath to come ; some point to law and to justice ; while others
breathe tones of love and mercy through a crucified Saviour, a
Divine Redeemer, and an all-prevailing Intercessor. Some in a
special manner direct the inquirer, comfort the mourner, and cheer
all who are in circumstances of affliction and distress. The value
and attraction of this volume will be increased by the diversity of
subjects and the heavenliness of their character. Some writers
have their faces flushed with the ardours of the eternal noon, and
their style wears the glow of that celestial sunshine : their pens
are dipped in love, the essence of which distils upon the mind, to
refreshen and invigorate, as the gentle rain descends upon the fields
of nature and the whole earth. The key-note to their sweetest
productions is the name of Jesus. His name is to them every-
where as an evergreen : it is hung on the walls of the mansion,
on the walls of the sick-chamber, on the walls of the nursery, on
the portals of the sanctuaries, and its choicest fragrance perfumes
their happiest homes.

What I seek, reader, is your benefit ; and, if the scattered fruit which
I have picked up in my researches enrich your spirit with a taste
of things Divine, it will compensate the time and patience I have
bestowed upon this work. To have been instrumental in allaying
the doubts of one inquirer, or in strengthening a believer in the
faith, would impart to my mind a joy which would baffle the
powers of a seraph to describe, and employ the ages of eternity
fully to tell. I have studiously avoided the insertion of any
compositions of sectarian tone. I wish to know no man after the
flesh ; but the more I know of the faithful in Christ Jesus, the more
I rejoice, and the more earnestly I pray that the walls of partition
may be thrown down, that uncharitable feelings may be suppressed,
that unity and concord may prevail in all our churches, that all the
followers of Christ may form one happy, united family, and faith-

fully to their profession and His cause rally round the Cross, till they become " clear as the moon, fair as the sun, and terrible as an army with banners."

By the death of one from whose writings I have made selections the church lost a faithful and devoted pastor, the city a wise, philanthropic, and public-spirited citizen, the college a learned and able professor, and all a common parent and friend. A feeling of sadness steals over the mind when we reflect upon the removal from earth of the brightest lights illuminating its murky atmosphere, luminaries which shone pre-eminently by the purity of their lustre. It is as if prisoners, whilst gazing from the windows of their cells on some narrow strip of sky, in which glittered a few friendly stars, beheld some envious vapours creep slowly along, quenching light after light, until they had spread a funeral pall over the entire range of vision, and left nothing to gaze upon but vacancy and gloom. But, in the mind of the Christian, this will be followed by thoughts of a more cheering character. He will presently remember with delight that what is thus lost to earth is gained to heaven. The lights have but changed their place, not forfeited their radiance. The hand of death has not extinguished them, but has only carried them to another apartment, where they stand on loftier pedestals and diffuse wider glory. Heaven is attracting to itself whatever is congenial to its nature, enriching itself by the spoils of earth, and collecting within its capacious bosom whatever is pure, permanent, and Divine. O that it may be given to us who remain behind rightly to improve these lessons addressed to us, that, loosening ourselves from the ties which bind us to the world, we may aspire with a holier fervour, and ascend with a steadier flight, to that land of life where all that is truly good, and great, and lovely shall at last be found. Suddenly and unexpectedly some of our writers were taken from earth ! in the midst of their work, in apparently unbroken health, with all their powers, both of mind and body, entire—cut down like some stately oak which at evening is seen casting its shadows afar across the sward, but, when the morning dawns, is found stripped of its foliage and stretched upon the soil. What a call to earnestness, to diligence, to preparation, to prayer ! O ye men of literature and science, ye votaries of wisdom and benevolence, ye senators, and sages, and philosophers! would that I could gather you around the tombs of these men, in whose genius your forefathers delighted, and to whose greatness they did homage, and there persuade you to listen to the lessons that issue thence, enforced by the whole course of their lives, proclaiming that all your science, and all your philosophy, and all your philanthropy, apart from love to God and faith in a crucified Redeemer, will prove but the idle day-dreams of a visionary enthusiasm, which shall melt, and perish, and be forgotten for ever. Be "followers of them who through faith and patience inherit the promises." Be wise, and work now for the honour and glory of God, for the salvation of immortal souls, and your reward will be great. "They that be wise shall shine as the brightness of the firmament; and they that turn many to righteousness as the stars for ever and ever."

It has been my aim that the same evangelical principles, the same fervent devotion, and the same truly Christian spirit by which the best poems are so eminently distinguished should characterize every part of this book.

I have scattered a few of my own compositions throughout the volume, and must beg that the mantle of charity may be thrown over all imperfections. I have made the book larger than I intended, and therefore have been obliged to increase the price. I beg most respectfully and sincerely to tender my cordial thanks to Sir ELKANAH ARMITAGE, Knt., for the honour he has done me in kindly granting his special permission to dedicate this volume to him. I am also much indebted to the Rev. HORATIUS BONAR, D.D., for kindly allowing me to insert several of his most beautiful poems; to the Hon. Rev. B. W. NOEL, M.A., Miss ELLIOTT, of Brighton, and "KATIE," for their kind permission and contributions; and all these, I trust, will accept this notice of my respectful and hearty thanks, and believe me to be their humble but faithful friend,

HENRY JENNINGS.

TADLEY, NEAR BASINGSTOKE,
December 1, 1864.

Contents.

Heavenly Melodies.

—·—o—·——

In every Trial Look Above.

FRIEND, why that look of sadness, care, and woe?
Why do those bitter tears so freely flow?
Art thou depress'd with grief?   Then look above,
Where all is joy, where all is peace and love ;
See there thy Father, God, enthroned in light.
Clothèd with majesty, with power and might :
The Judge, the King He is, the Lord of all ;
Before Him nations bow, the great, the small.
Thy burden now at once make known to Him :
He'll lighten every care, and cancel sin,
He'll whisper peace, reveal His lovely face,
And seal you for His child, an heir of grace.
Art thou a mourner reft of kindred dear ?
O, then, unto the mercy-seat draw near,

B

Behold by faith a Father in the skies,
Who feeds the poor and hears the orphan's cries.
Weep not for dear, for loved ones gone before:
They're happy now, and will be evermore;
They're robed in pure and spotless white,
And dwell in light, unfading, cloudless light;
They strike their harps in praise of love Divine,
And brighter as they sing for ever shine.
Of grace they sing, of free and matchless grace,
As they behold their Saviour face to face.
Press on, thou child of sorrow, higher rise,
To hail and meet thy loved ones in the skies,
Where cares no more shall cross thy peaceful breast,
But blest you'll be, yea, and for ever blest.

Henry Jennings.

Press On.

Be brave, my brother!
    Fight the good fight of faith
      With weapons proved and true;
    Be faithful and unshrinking to the death;
      Thy God will bear thee through.
    The strife is terrible,
      Yet 'tis not, 'tis not long;
    The foe is not invincible,
      Though fierce and strong.

Be brave, my brother!
  The recompense is great,
    The kingdom bright and fair;
  Beyond the glory of all earthly state
    Shall be the glory there.
  Grudge not the heavy cost,
    Faint not at labour here,
  'Tis but a lifetime at the most,
    The day of rest is near.

Be brave, my brother!
  He, whom thou servest, slights
    Not ev'n His weakest one;
  No deed, though poor, shall be forgot,
    However feebly done.
  The prayer, the wish, the thought,
    The faintly spoken word,
  The plan that seem'd to come to nought,
    Each has its own reward.

Be brave, my brother!
  Enlarge thy heart and soul;
    Spread out thy free, glad love;
  Encompass earth, embrace the sea,
    As does that sky above.
  Let no man see thee stand
    In slothful idleness,
  As if there were no work for thee
    In such a wilderness.

Be brave, my brother!
　Stint not the liberal hand;
　　Give, in the joy of love;
　So shall thy crown be bright, and great
　　Thy recompense above;
　Reward, not like the deed,
　　That poor, weak deed of thine,
　But like the God Himself who gives,
　　Eternal and Divine.

Horatius Bonar.

Cast your Care on Jesus.

Cast all your care on Jesus,
　Who died that you might live;
He'll bear your sins though weighty,
　He'll cancel and forgive.
Cast all your care on Jesus,
　Who lives again on high,
Who will from sin release you,
　And raise you to the sky.

Cast all your care on Jesus,
　Who loves to bless and save,
Who heal'd the blind, the lame,
　And freely mercy gave

Trust in God.

Cast all your care on Jesus,
  The best, the truest friend,
To your most simple cry
  He will most gladly bend.

Cast all your care on Jesus,
  He never will forsake,
But faithful and more faithful prove,
  For His own mercy sake.
Cast all your care on Jesus,
  Who did for sinners weep,
Whose bless'd Spirit sanctifies,
  And makes for glory meet.

Cast all your care on Jesus,
  Whose heart with pity moved,
Whose love for wretched man
  He has for ever proved.
Cast all your care on Jesus,
  Whose love should be proclaim'd,
Till ev'ry nation knows and loves
  The savour of His name.

Cast all your care on Jesus,
  Whose power can know no bound,
Whose praises will for ever
  In glorious song resound.
Cast all your care on Jesus,
  Whose promises stand fast,
Keep near Him when most tempted,
  Keep near Him to the last.

Cast all your care on Jesus,
   Whose blood for you was shed,
Who is for ever and for ever
   The Church's living head.
Cast all your care on Jesus,
   Who will His people keep,
And in their dying hour
   Will gently hush to sleep.

Cast all your care on Jesus,
   Who only can relieve
The heart so full of sorrow
   That thought can scarce conceive.
Cast all your care on Jesus,
   Who will relieve indeed
Your heart so fill'd with grief
   When suddenly bereaved.

Cast all your care on Jesus
   When weary and when sad,
And by His promised Spirit
   Your heart He will make glad.
Cast all your care on Jesus,
   Then will He say at last,
" Come in, thou blessed one, come in ;
   All storms are overpast."

Henry Jennings.

Trust in God.

Hoping in God.

O MY soul! what means this sadness?
　Wherefore art thou thus cast down?
Let thy griefs be turn'd to gladness,
　Bid thy restless fears be gone:
　　Look to Jesus,
And rejoice in His dear name.

What though Satan's strong temptations
　Vex and tease thee day by day,
And thy sinful inclinations
　Often fill thee with dismay?
　　Thou shalt conquer,
Through the Lamb's redeeming blood.

Though ten thousand ills beset thee
　From without and from within,
Jesus saith He'll ne'er forget thee,
　But will save from hell and sin;
　　He is faithful
To perform His gracious word.

Though distresses now attend thee,
　And thou tread'st the thorny road,
His right hand shall still defend thee,
　Soon He'll bring thee home to God:
　　Therefore praise Him,
Praise the great Redeemer's name.

O that I could now adore Him,
  Like the heavenly host above,
Who for ever bow before Him,
  And unceasing sing His love!
    Happy songsters!
When shall I your chorus join?

Fawcett.

Confidence in Jesus.

O HOLY Saviour, Friend unseen,
The faint, the weak, on Thee may lean:
Help me, throughout life's varying scene,
  By faith to cling to Thee!

Blest with communion so Divine,
Take what Thou wilt, shall I repine,
When, as the branches to the vine,
  My soul may cling to Thee?

Far from her home, fatigued, opprest,
Here she has found a place of rest,
An exile still, yet not unblest
  While she can cling to Thee!

Without a murmur I dismiss
My former dreams of earthly bliss;
My joy, my recompense be this,
  Each hour to cling to Thee!

What though the world deceitful prove,
And earthly friends and joys remove?
With patient, uncomplaining love
   Still would I cling to Thee!

Oft when I seem to tread alone
Some barren waste with thorns o'ergrown,
A voice of love, in gentlest tone,
   Whispers, "Still cling to Me!"

Though faith and hope awhile be tried,
I ask not, need not, aught beside:
How safe, how calm, how satisfied,
   The souls that cling to Thee!

They fear not life's rough storms to brave,
Since Thou art near, and strong to save;
Nor shudder e'en at death's dark wave,
   Because they cling to Thee!

Blest is my lot, whate'er befall:
What can disturb me, who appal,
While, as my strength, my rock, my all,
   Saviour! I cling to Thee?

            Charlotte Elliott.

Weak Faith.

Encompass'd with clouds of distress,
   Just ready all hope to resign,
I pant for the light of Thy face,
   And fear it will never be mine:

Dishearten'd with waiting so long,
   I sink at Thy feet with my load;
All plaintive I pour out my song,
   And stretch forth my hands unto God.

Shine, Lord, and my terror shall cease;
   The blood of atonement apply;
And lead me to Jesus for peace,—
   The Rock that is higher than I:
Speak, Saviour! for sweet is Thy voice:
   Thy presence is fair to behold:
Attend to my sorrows and cries—
   My groanings that cannot be told.

If sometimes I strive as I mourn
   My hold of Thy promise to keep,
The billows more fiercely return,
   And plunge me again in the deep:
While harass'd, and cast from Thy sight,
   The tempter suggests with a roar,—
"The Lord has forsaken thee quite;
   Thy God will be gracious no more."

Yet, Lord, if Thy love hath design'd
   No covenant blessing for me,
Ah, tell me how is it I find
   Some pleasure in waiting for Thee?
Almighty to rescue Thou art;
   Thy grace is my shield and my tower;
Come, succour and gladden my heart,—
   Let this be the day of Thy power.   *Anon.*

The Power of Faith.

FAITH adds new charms to earthly bliss,
   And saves me from its snares ;
Its aid in every duty brings,
   And softens all my cares :

Extinguishes the thirst for sin,
   And lights the sacred fire
Of love to God and heavenly things,
   And feeds the pure desire.

The wounded conscience knows its power
   The healing balm to give ;
That balm the saddest heart can cheer,
   And make the dying live.

Wide it unveils celestial worlds,
   Where deathless pleasures reign ;
And bids me seek my portion there,
   Nor bids me seek in vain :

Shows me the precious promise, seal'd
   With the Redeemer's blood ;
And helps my feeble hope to rest
   Upon a faithful God.

There, there unshaken would I rest
   Till this vile body dies ;
And then, on Faith's triumphant wings,
   At once to glory rise !

Turner.

Faith Triumphing.

A DEBTOR to mercy alone,
  Of covenant mercy I sing;
Nor fear, with Thy righteousness on,
  My person and offerings to bring:
The terrors of law and of God
  With me can have nothing to do;
My Saviour's obedience and blood
  Hide all my transgressions from view.

The work which His goodness began
  The arm of His strength will complete;
His promise is yea and amen,
  And never was forfeited yet:
Things future, nor things that are now,—
  Not all things below nor above,
Can make Him His purpose forego,
  Or sever my soul from His love.

My name from the palms of His hands
  Eternity will not erase;
Impress'd on His heart it remains
  In marks of indelible grace:
Yes, I to the end shall endure,
  As sure as the earnest is given;
More happy, but not more secure,
  The glorified spirits in heaven.

Toplady.

Trust in God.

Stability of Faith.

LORD, we lie before Thy feet :
  Look on all our deep distress ;
Thy rich mercy may we meet ;
  Clothe us with Thy righteousness ;
Stretch forth Thy almighty hand ;
Hold us up, and we shall stand.

O that closer we could cleave
  To Thy bleeding, dying breast !
Give us firmly to believe,
  And to enter into rest.
Lord, increase, increase our faith ;
Make us faithful unto death !

Let us trust Thee evermore ;
  Every moment on Thee call
For new life, new will, new power :
  Let us trust Thee, Lord, for all !
May we nothing know beside
Jesus, and Him crucified !

Hart.

Hope Thou in God.

WHY, when storms around you gather,
  Should your trembling spirits sink ?
Look to God, your heavenly Father,
  And of His sweet promise think.

Fancy will be often painting
    Scenes in dark and fearful shade,
Yet why should thy soul be fainting,
    Of prospective woes afraid?

Cease that dark anticipation,
    Still let love and faith abound;
For the day of tribulation
    Strength sufficient will be found.

God is love, and will not leave you,
    When you most His kindness need;
God is true, nor can deceive you,
    Though your faith be weak indeed.

Searle.

Return unto thy Rest.

CEASE, my soul, thy strayings!
    Have they brought thee peace?
Come, no more delayings,
    Cease thy wanderings, cease.
        These vanities how vain!
        Wander not again.

Thou hast found thy centre;
    There, my soul, abide;
Never more adventure
    Now to swerve aside.
        These vanities how vain!
        Wander not again.

Thou hast reach'd thy dwelling;
  Safe, sure anchorage
From the perilous swelling
  Of the tempest's rage.
      These vanities how vain !
      Wander not again.

Tranquil hours now greet thee
  In thy calm abode ;
Gracious looks now meet thee
  From thy loving God.
      These vanities how vain !
      Wander not again.

See, yon star, love-lighted,
  Sparkles from on high ;
See, yon hope, love-plighted,
  Cheers thy heaviest sky.
      These vanities how vain !
      Wander not again.

Watch, my soul, the glory
  Coming brightly up,
O'er yon forest hoary,
  O'er yon mountain-top.
      These vanities how vain !
      Wander not again.

'Tis the bridal morning ;
  Rise, make no delay ;

Put on thine adorning,
 Cast thy weeds away.
   These vanities how vain !
   Wander not again.

Pierce these mists that blind thee,
 Press to yonder prize,
Break the bonds that bind thee,
 Rise, my soul, arise !
   These vanities how vain !
   Wander not again.

      Horatius Bonar.

Ask, and Receive.

Jesus, the Friend of sinners, dear,
 Help me to love Thee more,
Give me Thy blessed Spirit now,
 That I may Thee adore.
Give me a contrite mind,
 A clean, a broken heart !
Write Thy holy law within,
 That I may ne'er depart.

Let thy word and Spirit dwell
 For ever in my breast ;
Yea, give me inward peace, O Lord,
 And grant me final rest.
Be thou my Guardian, Shepherd, Friend,
 Keep me by thy power,

Let no evil me attend
   In an unguarded hour.

Too often am I prone to stray,
   To leave the narrow way;
Forgive and pardon all my sins,
   Accept me now this day.
The merits of Thy Son I plead,
   The Lamb for sinners slain,
Who now for rebels intercedes,
   That they with Him may reign.

With boldness I approach and ask
   The blessings He has bought;
Clothe me with righteousness Divine,
   The garment He has wrought.
Sinful, weak, and frail I am,
   On Jesus I rely;
He is my strength, my portion all,
   And will be when I die.

I ask His presence now, but more
   In death's dark, latest hour;
Be with me, Saviour, Jesus dear,
   To break Satanic power.

Henry Jennings.

Trust in God.

DEAR Refuge of my weary soul!
   On Thee, when sorrows rise,
On Thee, when waves of trouble roll,
   My fainting hope relies.   c

To Thee I tell each rising grief,
　For Thou alone canst heal.
Thy word can bring a sweet relief
　For every pain I feel.

But, O when gloomy doubts prevail,
　I fear to call Thee mine :
The springs of comfort seem to fail,
　And all my hopes decline.

Yet, gracious God ! where shall I flee ?
　Thou art my only trust ;
And still my soul would cleave to Thee,
　Though prostrate in the dust.

Hast Thou not bid me seek Thy face ?
　And shall I seek in vain ?
And can the ear of sovereign grace
　Be deaf when I complain ?

No ! still the ear of sovereign grace
　Attends the mourner's prayer.
O may I ever find access,
　To breathe my sorrows there !

Thy mercy-seat is open still :
　There let my soul retreat ;
With humble hope attend Thy will,
　And wait beneath Thy feet.

Steele.

Free Salvation.

Jesus is our great salvation,
  Worthy of our best esteem ;
He has saved His favourite nation ;
  Join to sing aloud to Him ;
    He has saved us,
  Christ alone could us redeem.

When involved in sin and ruin,
  And no helper there was found,
Jesus our distress was viewing—
  Grace did more than sin abound ;
    He has called us,
  With salvation in the sound.

Save us from a mere profession !
  Save us from hypocrisy !
Give us, Lord, the sweet possession
  Of Thy righteousness and Thee :
    Best of favours !
  None compared with this can be.

Let us never, Lord, forget thee ;
  Make us walk as pilgrims here :
We will give Thee all the glory
  Of the love that brought us near ;
    Bid us praise Thee,
  And rejoice with holy fear.

Free election, known by calling,
    Is a privilege Divine :
Saints are kept from final falling ;
    All the glory, Lord, be Thine ;
      All the glory,
    All the glory, Lord, is Thine.   *Ano*

The Omnipotence of God.

Ye servants of your God, His fame
In songs of highest praise proclaim ;
Ye who, on His commands intent,
The courts of Israel's Lord frequent,

Him praise—the everlasting King,
And mercy's unexhausted spring :
Haste, to His name your voices rear ;
What name like His the heart can cheer ?

Thy greatness, Lord, my thoughts attest,
With awful gratitude imprest,
Nor know, among the seats Divine,
A power that shall contend with Thine :

O Thou, whose all-disposing sway
The heavens, the earth, and seas obey ;
Whose might through all extent extends,
Sinks through all depth, all height transcends ;

From earth's low margin to the skies,
Now bids the pregnant vapour rise ;
The lightning's pallid sheet expands,
And glads with showers the furrow'd lands ;

Now, from Thy storehouse, built on high,
Permits the imprison'd winds to fly,
And, guided by Thy will, to sweep
The surface of the foaming deep:

Him praise—the everlasting King,
And mercy's unexhausted spring:
Haste, to His name your voices rear;
What name like His the heart can cheer?

Merrick.

God the Creator.

The spacious firmament on high,
With all the blue ethereal sky,
And spangled heavens, a shining frame,
Their great Original proclaim.
The unwearied sun, from day to day,
Does his Creator's power display,
And publishes to every land
The work of an Almighty hand.

Soon as the evening shades prevail
The moon takes up the wondrous tale,
And nightly to the listening earth
Repeats the story of her birth;
Whilst all the stars that round her burn,
And all the planets in their turn,
Confirm the tidings, as they roll,
And spread the truth from pole to pole.

What though in solemn silence all
Move round the dark terrestrial ball ;
What though no real voice or sound
Amidst their radiant orbs be found ;
In reason's ear they all rejoice,
And utter forth a glorious voice,
For ever singing, as they shine,
"The hand that made us is Divine."

Addison.

God the Creator.

The Lord Jehovah reigns,
And royal state maintains,
His head with awful glories crown'd ;
Array'd robes in of light,
Begirt with sovereign might,
And rays of majesty around.

Upheld by Thy commands,
The world securely stands,
And skies and stars obey Thy word :
Thy throne was fix'd on high
Before the starry sky :
Eternal is Thy kingdom, Lord.

In vain the noisy crowd,
Like billows fierce and loud,
Against Thine empire rage and roar :

In vain, with angry spite,
The surly nations fight,
And dash like waves against the shore.

Let floods and nations rage,
And all their powers engage ;
Let swelling tides assault the sky :
The terrors of Thy frown
Shall beat their madness down :
Thy throne for ever stands on high.

Thy promises are true,
Thy grace is ever new ;
There fix'd, Thy Church shall ne'er remove :
Thy saints with holy fear
Shall in Thy courts appear,
And sing Thine everlasting love.

Isaac Watts.

The Wisdom of God.

WAIT, O my soul, thy Maker's will ;
Tumultuous passions, all be still ;
Nor let a murmuring thought arise !
His ways are just, His counsels wise.

He in the thickest darkness dwells,
Performs His work, the cause conceals :
But, though His methods are unknown,
Judgment and truth support His throne.

In heaven, and earth, and air, and seas
He executes His firm decrees;
And by His saints it stands confess'd
That what He does is ever best.

Wait, then, my soul, submissive wait,
Prostrate before His awful seat;
And, 'midst the terrors of His rod,
Trust in a wise and gracious God.

Beddome.

Providence Wise and Good.

Thy ways, O Lord! with wise design,
Are framed upon Thy throne above,
And every dark and bending line
Meets in the centre of Thy love.

With feeble light and half obscure,
Poor mortals thy arrangements view;
Not knowing that the least are sure,
And the mysterious just and true.

Thy flock, Thy own peculiar care,
Though now they seem to roam uneyed,
Are led or driven only where
They best and safest may abide.

They neither know nor trace the way:
But, trusting to Thy piercing eye,
None of their feet to ruin stray,
Nor shall the weakest fail or die.

My favour'd soul shall meekly learn
To lay her reason at Thy throne;
Too weak Thy secrets to discern,
I'll trust Thee for my guide alone.

Searle.

Creation and Providence.

LORD, when our raptured thought surveys
   Creation's beauties o'er,
All nature joins to teach Thy praise,
   And bid our souls adore.

Where'er we turn our gazing eyes,
   Thy radiant footsteps shine;
Ten thousand pleasing wonders rise,
   And speak their source Divine.

The living tribes of countless forms
   In earth, and sea, and air,
The meanest flies, the smallest worms,
   Almighty power declare.

Thy wisdom, power, and goodness, Lord,
   In all Thy works appear:
And, oh! let man Thy praise record,—
   Man, Thy distinguish'd care!

From Thee the breath of life he drew;
   That breath Thy power maintains;
Thy tender mercy, ever new,
   His brittle frame sustains.

Yet nobler favours claim his praise,
   Of reason's light possess'd ;
By revelation's brightest rays
   Still more divinely bless'd.

Thy providence his constant guard
   When threat'ning woes impend,
Or will th'. impending dangers ward,
   Or timely succours lend.

On us that providence has shone
   With gentle smiling rays :
O may our lips and lives make known
   Thy goodness and Thy praise!

Steele.

God's Goodness.

Ye sons of men, with joy record
The various wonders of the Lord,
And let His power and goodness sound
Through all your tribes the earth around.

Let the high heavens your songs invite,
Those spacious fields of brilliant light,
Where sun, and moon, and planets roll,
And stars that glow from pole to pole.

Sing earth, in verdant robes array'd—
Its herbs and flowers, its fruit and shade ;
Peopled with life of various forms,
Of fish, and fowl, and beasts, and worms.

View the broad sea's majestic plains,
And think how wide its Maker reigns;
That band remotest nations joins,
And on each wave His goodness shines.

But O that brighter world above,
Where lives and reigns incarnate love!
God's only Son, in flesh array'd,
For man a bleeding victim made.

Thither, my soul, with rapture soar!
There, in the land of praise adore:
The theme demands an angel's lay—
Demands an everlasting day.

Doddridge.

A Song of Praise.

O FOR a thankful, grateful heart,
    To sing my Saviour's praise,
To celebrate His wondrous love,
    In nobler, sweeter lays!

How great His love in rescuing me
    From sin and death and hell;
His mercy still so rich and free
    I will to sinners tell.

He raised me from the miry clay,
    And led my wandering feet
Along the straight and narrow way,
    E'en to the mercy-seat.

He bless'd me with His Spirit there,
  And taught me how to pray,
And will still bless me more and more,
  If I ask day by day.

He keeps me by His mighty hand,
  And on Him I rely,
For every blessing which He gives,
  In life, and when I die.

He helps me too when sore oppress'd,
  I'm ever in His sight,
He makes me meet my strongest foes,
  And puts them all to flight.

He nerves me for the conflict great,
  And drives my fears away,
In His own strength I conquer still,
  And shall from day to day.

He ever cheers me by His grace,
  When sorrow fills my breast,
And says, " Come home, thou weary one,
  And I will give thee rest."

He writes my name in His own book,
  His name upon my heart ;
Assures me of His faithfulness,
  That we shall never part.

His praises I will loudly sing,
  Until He bids me rise,
To join with rapture and with love
  The armies in the skies.

Henry Jennings.

Faith.

On wings of faith mount up, my soul, and rise ;
View thine inheritance beyond the skies.
Nor heart can think, nor mortal tongue can tell,
What endless pleasures in those mansions dwell.
There our Redeemer lives, all bright and glorious :
O'er sin, and death, and hell, He reigns victorious.

No gnawing grief, no sad, heart-rending pain,
In that blest country can admission gain ;
No sorrow there, no soul-tormenting fear,
For God's own hand shall wipe the falling tear :
There our Redeemer lives, all bright and glorious :
O'er sin, and death, and hell, He reigns victorious.

Before the throne a crystal river glides ;
Immortal verdure decks its cheerful sides :
There the fair tree of life majestic rears
Its blooming head, and sovereign virtue bears.
There our Redeemer lives, all bright and glorious :
O'er sin, and death, and hell, He reigns victorious.

No rising sun his needless beams displays ;
No sickly moon emits her feeble rays.
The Godhead there celestial glory sheds :
The exalted Lamb eternal radiance spreads.
There our Redeemer lives, all bright and glorious :
O'er sin, and death, and hell, He reigns victorious.

The distant glimpse my eager passion fires :
Jesus ! to Thee my longing soul aspires !
When shall I at Thy heavenly home arrive ?
When leave this earth, and when begin to live ?
There is my Saviour seen, all bright and glorious :
O'er sin, and death, and hell, He reigns victorious.

Strachan.

Faith's Review and Expectation.

AMAZING grace ! how sweet the sound,
  That saved a wretch like me !
I once was lost, but now am found,
  Was blind, but now I see.

'Twas grace that taught my heart to fear,
  And grace my fears relieved :
How precious did that grace appear
  The hour I first believed !

Through many dangers, toils, and snares,
  I have already come :
'Tis grace has brought me safe thus far,
  And grace will lead me home.

The Lord has promised good to me,
  His word my hope secures ;
He will my shield and portion be,
  As long as life endures.

Yes, when this flesh and heart shall fail,
  And mortal life shall cease,
I shall possess, within the veil,
  A life of joy and peace.

The earth shall soon dissolve like snow,
  The sun forbear to shine,
But God, who call'd me here below,
  Will be for ever mine.

Newton

The Influence of Faith.

When faith presents the Saviour's death,
  And whispers " This is thine,"
Sweetly my rising hours advance,
  And peacefully decline.

While such my views, the radiant sun
  Sheds a more sprightly ray;
Each object smiles, all nature charms;
  I sing my cares away.

Hervey.

The Confidence of Faith.

Jesus is mine! I'm now prepared
To meet with what I thought most hard;
Yes, let the winds of trouble blow,
And comforts melt away like snow:

No blasted trees or failing crops
  Can hinder my eternal hopes ;
Though creatures change, the Lord 's the same ;
  Then let me triumph in His name.
Newton.

My Soul thirsteth for God.

I THIRST, but not as once I did,
  The vain delights of earth to share :
Thy wounds, Emmanuel ! all forbid
  That I should seek my pleasures there.

It was the sight of Thy dear cross
  First wean'd my soul from earthly things,
And taught me to esteem as dross
  The mirth of fools and pomp of kings.

I want that grace that springs from Thee,
  That quickens all things where it flows.
And makes a wretched thorn like me
  Bloom as the myrtle or the rose.

Dear Fountain of delight unknown !
  No longer sink below the brim ;
But overflow, and pour me down
  A living and life-giving stream !

For sure, of all the plants that share
  The notice of thy Father's eye,
None proves less grateful to His care,
  Or yields Him meaner fruit, than I.
Cowper.

Faith.

O HAPPY day, that fix'd my choice
   On Thee, my Saviour and my God!
Well may this glowing heart rejoice,
   And tell its raptures all abroad.

O happy bond, that seals my vows
   To Him who merits all my love!
Let cheerful anthems fill His house,
   While to that sacred shrine I move.

'Tis done; the great transaction's done;
   I am my Lord's, and He is mine.
He drew me, and I followed on,
   Glad to confess the voice Divine.

Now rest, my long-divided heart;
   Fix'd on this blissful centre, rest:
With ashes who would grudge to part,
   When called on angels' bread to feast?

High Heaven, that heard the solemn vow,
   That vow renew'd shall daily hear;
Till in life's latest hour I bow,
   And bless in death a bond so dear.

Doddridge.

D

Seed-time, and Joyful Harvest.

The darken'd sky, how thick it low'rs!
Troubled with storms and big with show'rs;
No cheerful gleam of light appears,
But Nature pours forth all her tears.

Yet let the sons of grace revive;
God bids the soul that seeks Him live;
And from the gloomiest shade of night
Calls forth a morning of delight.

The seeds of ecstasy unknown
Are in these water'd furrows sown;
See the green blades, how thick they rise,
And with fresh verdure bless our eyes.

In secret foldings they contain
Unnumber'd ears of golden grain;
And heav'n shall pour its beams around,
Till the ripe harvest load the ground.

Then shall the trembling mourner come,
And find his sheaves and bear them home;
The voice long broke with sighs shall sing,
Till heav'n with hallelujahs ring.

Doddridge.

Hope in Affliction.

WHEN musing sorrow weeps the past,
　And mourns the present pain,
'Tis sweet to think of peace at last,
　And feel that death is gain.

'Tis not that murm'ring thoughts arise,
　And dread a Father's will;
'Tis not that meek submission flies,
　And would not suffer still.

It is that heav'n-born Faith surveys
　The path that leads to light,
And longs her eagle-plumes to raise,
　And lose herself in sight.

It is that hope with ardour glows
　To see Him face to face,
Whose dying love no language knows
　Sufficient art to trace.

It is that harass'd conscience feels
　The pangs of struggling sin,
And sees, though far, the hand that heals
　And ends the strife within.

O let me wing my hallow'd flight
　From earth-born woe and care,
And soar above these clouds of night,
　My Saviour's bliss to share!

Cotterill's Sel.

D 2

Hope of Day.

TILL the day dawn,
And the Day-star arise,
  Father, O keep Thy son,
  Thy feeble, faithless one!
  O guide him through the waste,
  Till the long gloom be past!
  It is a night of fear;
  The path is rough and drear;
  Clouds frown, blasts rush along,
  The tempests gather strong;
  Strange perils compass me,
  Of flood, fire, rock, and sea;
  Yet I, in loneliness,
  Would fain still onward press.
O felt and known, but yet unseen, be nigh;
O loved and longed for, hear each hidden sigh:
Leave me not, struggling thus, to sink and die.

Till the day dawn,
And the Day-star arise,
  O Saviour, let Thy love,
  Down-dropping from above,
  This wither'd soul renew
  With Thy flower-freshening dew!
  O never-changing Friend,
  My failing steps attend;

Hold Thou me up, and so
I shall pass safely through.
Still keep me at Thy side,
Thou who for me hast died.
O light me on my way,
My joy, my strength, my stay!
O clasp me closer to Thy piercèd side,
Thou who for me the death of deaths hast died!
Let not this staggering faith be too, too sorely
tried.

Till the day dawn,
And the Day-star arise,
Spirit of gentle love,
Thou tempest-calming Dove,
Come, and within me dwell,
Come, and all gloom dispel.
Most blessed Comforter,
My weary footsteps cheer.
O light and lamp Divine,
Upon my midnight shine;
Better than star or moon,
Brighter than day's bright noon,
O let Thy joyous ray
Turn all my night to day!
When Thou art absent, even my joy is sad;
When Thou art with me, even my grief is glad:
Let not Thy silence now sorrow to sorrow add.

Till the day dawn,
And the Day-star arise,
  Church of the living God,
  Pursue thy upward road;
  Look not behind, nor stray
  From the well-trodden way.
  Be not ashamed to bear
  Thy cross on earth, nor fear
  Reproach and poverty
  For Him who died for thee.
  With girded loins press on,
  Till the reward is won.
  Think of thy absent Lord;
  Hold fast thy plighted word.
Doff not thy weeds of widowhood, nor fear
To let the world through which thou passest hear
The widow's cry, and see the widow's faithful tear.

Horatius Bonar.

Supreme Love to Christ.

My gracious Redeemer I love!
His praises aloud I'll proclaim,
And join with the armies above
To shout His adorable name:
To gaze on His glories Divine
Shall be my eternal employ,
And feel them incessantly shine,
My boundless, ineffable joy.

He freely redeem'd with His blood
My soul from the confines of hell,
To live on the smiles of my God,
And in His sweet presence to dwell;
To shine with the angels of light,
With saints and with seraphs to sing;
To view with eternal delight
My Jesus, my Saviour, my King.

In Meshech as yet I reside,
A darksome and restless abode!
Molested with foes on each side,
And longing to dwell with my God.
O when shall my spirit exchange
This cell of corruptible clay
For mansions celestial, and range
Through realms of ineffable day?

My glorious Redeemer! I long
To see Thee descend on the cloud,
Amidst the bright, numberless throng,
And mix with the triumphing crowd.
O when wilt Thou bid me ascend,
To join in Thy praises above,
To gaze on Thee, world without end,
And feast on Thy ravishing love?

Nor sorrow, nor sickness, nor pain,
Nor sin, nor temptation, nor fear,
Shall ever molest me again,—
Perfection of glory reigns there:

This soul and this body shall shine
In robes of salvation and praise,
And banquet on pleasures Divine,
Where God His full beauty displays.

Ye palaces, sceptres, and crowns,
Your pride with disdain I survey;
Your pomps are but shadows and sounds,
And pass in a moment away:
The crown that my Saviour bestows
Yon permanent sun shall outshine;
My joy everlastingly flows,—
My God, my Redeemer, is mine.

Francis.

The Love of Jesus.

Jesus, Thy love exceeds by far
　　The love of earthly friends,
Bestows all that the sinner needs,
　　And never, never ends.

Thy love is boundless and 'tis free;
　　Its riches none can tell,
Till they ascend to Thy right hand,
　　Where saints for ever dwell.

No balm like this for all our woes;
　　It makes us ever blest;
It calms the troubled, anxious soul,
　　And gives the weary rest.

The greatest sinners feel its power :
    They worship, love, adore.
O for a thankful, grateful heart,
    To love Thee more and more !

Thy love demands the noblest song—
    Such songs as angels raise.
Come, Holy Spirit, come and tune
    Our hearts to sweetest praise.

Henry Jennings.

Perfect Love.

THAT perfect love is perfect bliss,
    Proof rises all around ;
Nor shall felicity but this
    In earth or heaven be found.

This is the joy of joy, I know,
    That can delight impart ;
Warm as the ruby tides that flow
    Incessant from my heart.

This is the joy that angels feel,
    Where harps celestial move ;
And the fierce anguish known in hell
    Is perfect want of love !

Say—is not this the dazzling light
    That decks the seraph's crown ?
What is perdition's tenfold night
    But love's eternal frown ?

Saffery.

Longing to Love Christ.

I thirst, Thou wounded Lamb of God,
To wash me in Thy cleansing blood,
To dwell within Thy wounds; then pain
Is sweet, and life or death is gain.

Take my poor heart, and let it be
For ever closed to all but Thee!
Seal Thou my breast, and let me wear
That pledge of love for ever there!

How blest are they who still abide
Close shelter'd in Thy bleeding side!
Who life and strength from thence derive,
And by Thee move, and in Thee live.

What are our works but sin and death,
Till Thou Thy quick'ning Spirit breathe?
Thou giv'st the power Thy grace to move:
O wondrous grace! O boundless love!

How can it be, Thou heavenly King,
That Thou shouldst us to glory bring—
Make slaves the partners of Thy throne,
Deck'd with a never-fading crown?

Hence our hearts melt; our eyes o'erflow;
Our words are lost; nor will we know,
Nor will we think of aught beside,
"My Lord, my Love, is crucified."

Ah, Lord! enlarge our scanty thought,
To know the wonders Thou hast wrought;
Unloose our stammering tongues, to tell
Thy love immense, unsearchable.

First-born of many brethren Thou!
To Thee, lo! all our souls we bow:
To Thee our hearts and hands we give:
Thine may we die; Thine may we live.

Wesley.

One in Christ.

COMPARED with Christ, in all beside
  No comeliness I see;
The one thing needful, dearest Lord,
  Is to be one with Thee.
The sense of Thy expiring love
  Into my soul convey;
Thyself bestow: for Thee alone
  I absolutely pray.

Whatever else Thy will withholds,
  Here grant me to succeed!
O let Thyself my portion be,
  And I am blest indeed!
Less than Thyself will not suffice
  My comfort to restore;
More than Thyself I cannot have,
  And Thou canst give no more.

Loved of my God, for Him again
   With love intense I burn ;
Chosen of Thee ere time began,
   I choose Thee in return !
Whate'er consists not with Thy love,
   O teach me to resign !
I'm rich to all th' intents of bliss,
   If Thou, O God, art mine !

Toplady.

𝕳𝖆𝖕𝖕𝖞 𝖎𝖓 𝖙𝖍𝖊 𝕷𝖔𝖛𝖊 𝖔𝖋 𝕵𝖊𝖘𝖚𝖘.

ETERNAL God, of beings First,
   Of all created good the Spring,
For Thee I long, for Thee I thirst,
   My Love, my Saviour, and my King !
Thine is a never-failing store ;
If God be mine, I ask no more.

The fairest world of light on high
   Reflection makes but faint of Thine ;
The glorious tenants of the sky
   In God's own beams transported shine :
But, shouldst Thou wrap Thy face in shade,
Soon all their life and lustre fade.

Thy Presence makes celestial day,
   And fills each raptured soul with bliss ;
Night would prevail were God away,
   And spirits pine in Paradise !

In vain would all the angels try
To fill Thy room, Thy lack supply.

And, sure, from Heav'n we turn our eyes
   In vain, to seek for bliss below ;
The tree of Life can't root nor rise,
   Nor in this blasted region grow :
The wealth of this poor barren clod
Can ne'er make up the want of God.

But, Lord, in Thee the thirsty soul
   Will meet with full, with rich supplies !
Thy smiles will all her fears control,
   Thy beauties feast her ravish'd eyes :
To failing flesh and fainting hearts
Thy favour life and strength imparts !

Simon Browne.

The Elder Brother.

Yes, for me, for me He careth
   With a brother's tender care :
Yes, with me, with me He shareth
   Every burden, every fear.

Yes, o'er me, o'er me He watcheth,
   Ceaseless watcheth, night and day :
Yes, even me, even me He snatcheth
   From the perils of the way.

Yes, for me He standeth pleading
   At the mercy-seat above;
Ever for me interceding,
   Constant in untiring love.

Yes, in me abroad He sheddeth
   Joys unearthly, love and light;
And to cover me He spreadeth
   His paternal wing of night.

Yes, in me, in me He dwelleth;
   I in Him and He in me!
And my empty soul He filleth,
   Here and through eternity.

Thus I wait for His returning,
   Singing all the way to heaven;
Such the joyful song of morning,
   Such the tranquil song of even.

               Horatius Bonar.

Ever Near.

I CLOSE my heavy eye,
   Saviour, ever near!
I lift my soul on high
   Through the darkness drear.
Be Thou my light, I cry,
   Saviour, ever dear!

I feel Thine arms around,
    Saviour, ever near!
With Thee let me be found;
    So shall I never fear,
Whatever ills abound,
    Saviour, ever dear!

Thine is the day and night,
    Saviour, ever near!
Thine is the dark and light;
    Be thou my covert here:
O shield me with Thy might,
    Saviour, ever dear!

And when I come to die,
    Saviour, ever near,
Receive my parting sigh;
    And in the hour of fear
Be to my spirit nigh,
    Saviour, ever dear!

Horatius Bonar.

The Name of Names.

FATHER, Thy Son hath died
    The sinner's death of woe;
Stooping in love from heaven to earth,
    Our curse to undergo;

Our curse to undergo,
  Upon the hateful tree.
Give glory to Thy Son, O Lord,
Put honour on that name of names
  By blessing me !

Father, Thy Son hath borne
  The sinner's doom of shame ;
Bearing His cross without the gate,
  He met the law's full claim ;
  He met the law's full claim,
    Sin's righteous penalty.
Give glory to Thy Son, O Lord,
Put honour on that name of names
  By pardoning me !

Father, Thy Son hath pour'd
  His life-blood on this earth,
To cleanse away our guilt and stains,
  To give us second birth ;
  To give us second birth,
    From sin to set us free.
Give glory to Thy Son, O Lord,
Put honour on that name of names
  By cleansing me !

For us He earn'd the bliss ;
  Amen, so let it be !
Give glory to Thy Son, O Lord,
Put honour on that name of names
  By crowning me !   *Horatius Bonar.*

The Joy of the Lord is our Strength.

Joy is a fruit that will not grow
    In nature's barren soil :
All we can boast, till Christ we know,
    Is vanity and toil.

But where the Lord has planted grace,
    And made His glories known,
There fruits of heav'nly joy and peace
    Are found, and there alone.

A bleeding Saviour seen by faith,
    A sense of pard'ning love,
A hope that triumphs over death,
    Give joys like those above.

To take a glimpse within the veil,
    To know that God is mine,
Are springs of joy that never fail,
    Unspeakable ! Divine !

These are the joys which satisfy
    And sanctify the mind;
Which make the spirit mount on high,
    And leave the world behind.

No more, believers, mourn your lot,
    But, if you are the Lord's,
Resign to them that know Him not
    Such joys as earth affords.

Newton.

E

Rejoicing in God.

THE righteous Lord, supremely great,
Maintains His universal state;
O'er all the earth His pow'r extends;
All heav'n before His footstool bends.

Yet justice still with pow'r presides,
And mercy all His empire guides;
Such works are pleasing in His sight,
And such the men of His delight.

No more, ye wise, your wisdom boast;
No more, ye strong, your valour trust;
Nor let the rich survey his store,
Elate with heaps of shining ore.

Glory, my soul, in this alone,
That God—thy God—to thee is known,
That thou hast own'd His sov'reign sway,
That thou hast felt His cheering ray.

My wisdom, wealth, and pow'r I find
In one Jehovah all combined!
On Him I fix my roving eyes,
Till all my soul in rapture rise.

All else, which I my treasure call,
May in one fatal moment fall;
But what his happiness can move
Whom God the blessed deigns to love?

Doddridge.

Rejoicing in God.

So firm the saint's foundations stand,
  Nor can his hopes remove,
Sustain'd by God's almighty hand,
  And shelter'd in His love.

Fig-trees and olive-plants may fail,
  And vines their fruit deny,
Famine through all his fields prevail,
  And flocks and herds may die:

God is the treasure of his soul,
  A source of sacred joy,
Which no afflictions can control,
  Nor death itself destroy.

Lord, may we feel Thy cheering beams,
  And taste Thy saints' repose;
We will not mourn the perish'd streams
  While such a fountain flows.

Doddridge.

Having the Son, and Life in Him.

O HAPPY Christian, who can boast,
  "The Son of God is mine!"
Happy, though humbled in the dust,
  Rich in this gift Divine

He lives the life of heav'n below,
  And shall for ever live;
Eternal streams from Christ shall flow,
  And endless vigour give.

E 2

That life we ask, with bended knee,
  Nor will the Lord deny ;
Nor will celestial mercy see
  Its humble suppliants die.

That life obtain'd, for praise alone
  We wish continued breath,
And, taught by blest experience, own
  That praise can live in death.

Doddridge.

The Happy Change.

How blest Thy creature is, O God,
  When with a single eye
He views the lustre of Thy word,
  The day-spring from on high !

Through all the storms that veil the skies,
  And frowns on earthly things,
The Sun of Righteousness he eyes,
  With healing on His wings.

Struck by that light, the human heart,
  A barren soil no more,
Sends the sweet smell of grace abroad,
  Where serpents lurk'd before.

The soul, a dreary province once
  Of Satan's dark domain,
Feels a new empire form'd within,
  And owns a heav'nly reign.

Joy.

The glorious orb, whose golden beams
  The fruitful year control,
Since first, obedient to Thy word,
  He started from the goal,

Has cheer'd the nations with the joys
  His orient rays impart;
But, Jesus! 'tis Thy light alone
  Can shine upon the heart.

Cowper.

Peace in Christ.

Thou very present aid
  In suffering and distress,
The soul which still on Thee is stay'd
  Is kept in perfect peace.
  The soul, by faith reclined
  On the Redeemer's breast,
'Mid raging storms exults to find
  An everlasting rest.

Sorrow and fear are gone
  Whene'er Thy face appears:
It stills the sighing orphan's moan,
  And dries the widow's tears.
  It hallows every cross;
  It sweetly comforts me,
Makes me forget my every loss,
  And find my all in Thee.

Jesus, to whom I fly,
   Doth all my wishes fill.
What though created streams are dry ?
   I have the Fountain still.
Stripp'd of my early friends,
   I find them all in *One;*
And peace, and joy that never ends,
   And heaven in Christ begun.

C. Wesley.

Let us Exalt His Name together.

GREAT the joy when Christians meet !
Christian fellowship, how sweet,
When, their theme of praise the same,
They exalt Jehovah's name !

Sing we then eternal love ;
Such as did the Father move.
He beheld the world undone ;
Loved the world, and gave His Son.

Sing the Son's unbounded love ;
How He left the realms above ;
Took our nature and our place ;
Lived and died to save our race.

Sing we, too, the Spirit's love :
With our stubborn hearts He strove ;
Chased the mists of sin away ;
Turn'd our night to glorious day.

Joy.

Great the joy, the union sweet,
When the saints in glory meet;
Where the theme is still the same,
Where they praise Jehovah's name.

G. Burder.

The Saint Indeed.

Happy the man whose cautious steps
    Still keep the golden mean;
Whose life, by wisdom's rules well form'd,
    Declares a conscience clean.

Not of himself he highly thinks,
    Nor acts the boaster's part:
His modest tongue the language speaks
    Of his still humbler heart.

Not in base scandal's arts he deals,
    For truth dwells in his breast;
With grief he sees his neighbour's faults,
    And thinks and hopes the best.

What blessings bounteous Heaven bestows
    He takes with thankful heart;
With temp'rance he both eats and drinks,
    And gives the poor a part.

To sect or party his large soul
    Disdains to be confined;
The good he loves of every name,
    And prays for all mankind.

Pure is his zeal, the offspring fair
   Of truth and heavenly love;
The bigot's rage can never dwell
   Where rests the peaceful dove.

His business is to keep his heart,
   Each passion to control;
Nobly ambitious well to rule
   The empire of his soul.

Not on the world his heart is set;
   His treasure is above:
Nothing beneath the sovereign good
   Can claim his highest love.

Needham.

The Spiritual Pilgrim.

How happy is the pilgrim's lot!
How free from anxious care and thought,
   From worldly hope and fear!
Confined to neither court nor cell,
His soul disdains on earth to dwell:
   He only sojourns here.

His happiness in part is mine:
Already saved from self design,
   From every creature-love—
Bless'd with the scorn of finite good—
My soul is lighten'd of its load,
   And seeks the things above.

Joy.

The things eternal I pursue,
And happiness beyond the view
   Of those who basely pant
For things by nature felt and seen :
Their honours, wealth, and pleasures mean
   I neither have nor want.

Nothing on earth I call my own :
A stranger to the world unknown,
   I all their goods despise ;
I trample on their whole delight,
And seek a country out of sight,
   A country in the skies.

There are my house and portion fair
My treasure and my heart are there,
   And my abiding home :
For me my elder brethren stay,
And angels beckon me away,
   And Jesus bids me come.

I come, Thy servant, Lord, replies ;
I come to meet Thee in the skies,
   And claim my heavenly rest :
Now let the pilgrim's journey end,
Now, O my Saviour, Brother, Friend,
   Receive me to Thy breast !

Wesley.

Welcoming the Cross.

'Tis my happiness below
  Not to live without the cross;
But the Saviour's power to know,
  Sanctifying every loss:
Trials must and will befall;
  But—with humble faith to see
Love inscribed upon them all—
  This is happiness to me.

God, in Israel, sows the seeds
  Of affliction, pain, and toil;
These spring up and choke the weeds
  Which would else o'erspread the soil:
Trials make the promise sweet;
  Trials give new life to prayer;
Trials bring me to His feet,
  Lay me low, and keep me there.

Did I meet no trials here—
  No chastisement by the way—
Might I not, with reason, fear
  I should prove a castaway?
Bastards may escape the rod,
  Sunk in earthly vain delight;
But the true-born child of God
  Must not—would not if he might.

Cowper.

The Lost Found; or, Joy in Heaven.

WHEN some kind shepherd from his fold
   Has lost a straying sheep,
Through vales, o'er hills, he anxious roves,
   And climbs the mountain's steep:

But O the joy! the transport sweet,
   When he the wanderer finds!
Up in his arms he takes his charge,
   And to his shoulders binds.

Homeward he hastes to tell his joys,
   And make his bliss complete:
The neighbours hear the news, and all
   The joyful shepherd greet.

Yet how much greater is the joy
   When but one sinner turns;
When the poor wretch, with broken heart,
   His sins and errors mourns!

Pleased with the news, the saints below
   In songs their tongues employ;
Beyond the skies the tidings go,
   And heaven is fill'd with joy.

Well pleased, the Father sees and hears
   The conscious sinner weep;
Jesus receives him in His arms,
   And owns him for His sheep.

Nor angels can their joys contain,
   But kindle with new fire:
" A wandering sheep 's return'd," they sing,
   And strike the sounding lyre.

Anon.

The Riches of Pardoning Grace.

Let heav'n burst forth into a song;
Let earth reflect the joyful sound;
Ye mountains, with the echo ring,
And shout, ye forests all around.

The Lord His Israel hath redeem'd,
Hath made His mourning people glad,
And the rich glories of His name
In their salvation hath display'd.

Unnumber'd sins, like sable clouds,
Veil'd ev'ry cheerful ray of joy,
And thunders murmur'd through the gloom,
While lightnings pointed to destroy.

He spoke, and all the clouds dispersed,
And heav'n unveil'd its shining face;
The whole creation smiled anew,
Deck'd in the golden beams of grace.

Israel, return in humble love,
Return to thy Redeemer's breast,
And, charm'd by His melodious voice,
Compose thy weary powers to rest.   Doddridge.

𝔓𝔞𝔯𝔡𝔬𝔫 𝔖𝔭𝔬𝔨𝔢𝔫 𝔟𝔶 ℭ𝔥𝔯𝔦𝔰𝔱.

My Saviour, let me hear Thy voice
    Pronounce these words of peace,
And all my warmest pow'rs shall join
    To celebrate Thy grace.

With gentle smiles call me Thy child,
    And speak my sins forgiv'n ;
The accents mild shall charm mine ear
    All like the harps of heav'n.

Cheerful, where'er Thy hand shall lead,
    The darkest path I'll tread ;
Cheerful I'll quit these mortal shores,
    And mingle with the dead.

When dreadful guilt is done away
    No other fears we know :
That hand that scatters pardons down,
    Shall crowns of life bestow.
                            Doddridge.

𝔇𝔦𝔳𝔦𝔫𝔢 𝔉𝔬𝔯𝔤𝔦𝔳𝔢𝔫𝔢𝔰𝔰.

Forgiveness ! 'tis a joyful sound
To malefactors doomed to die :
Publish the bliss the world around ;
Ye seraphs, shout it from the sky !

'Tis the rich gift of love Divine;
'Tis full, out-meas'ring every crime:
Unclouded shall its glories shine,
And feel no change by changing time.

O'er sins unnumber'd as the sand,
And like the mountains for their size,
The seas of sov'reign grace expand,
The seas of sov'reign grace arise.

For this stupendous love of Heaven
What grateful honours shall we show?
Where much transgression is forgiv'n
Let love in equal ardours glow.

By this inspired, let all our days
With various holiness be crown'd;
Let truth and goodness, pray'r and praise,
In all abide, in all abound.

Gibbons.

Israel Invited to Return to God.

Backsliding Israel, hear the voice
    Of thy forgiving God,
Nor force such goodness to exert
    The terrors of the rod.

Thus saith the Lord: " My mercy flows
    An unexhausted stream;
And, after all its millions saved,
    Its sway is still supreme.

" One moment's wrath, with weighty crush,
    Might sink you quick to hell;
Yet mercy points the happy path
    Where life and glory dwell.

" Own but the follies thou hast done,
    And mourn thy sins in dust,
And soon thy trembling heart shall learn
    To hope, and love, and trust."

All-gracious God, Thy voice we own;
    And, prostrate at Thy feet,
Our souls in humble silence wait
    A pardon there to meet.

                            Doddridge.

The Backslider, etc.

THE Lord, how kind are all His ways,
    When most they seem severe !
He frowns, and scourges, and rebukes,
    That we may learn His fear.

With thorns He fences up our path,
    And builds a wall around,
To guard us from the death that lurks
    In sin's forbidden ground.

When other lovers, sought in vain,
    Our fond address despise,
He opens His indulgent arms,
    With pity in His eyes.

Return, ye wand'ring souls, return,
  And seek His tender breast;
Call back the mem'ry of the days
  When there you found your rest.

Behold, O Lord, we fly to Thee,
  Though blushes veil our face,
Constrain'd our last retreat to seek
  In Thy much-injured grace.

                                  Doddridge.

God Speaking Peace to His People.

Unite, my roving thoughts, unite
  In silence soft and sweet;
And thou, my soul, sit gently down
  At thy great Sovereign's feet.

Jehovah's awful voice is heard,
  Yet gladly I attend:
For, lo! the everlasting God
  Proclaims Himself my Friend.

Harmonious accents to my soul
  The sounds of peace convey:
The tempest at His word subsides,
  And winds and seas obey.

By all its joys, I charge my heart
  To grieve His love no more;
But, charm'd by melody Divine,
  To give its follies o'er.   *Doddridge.*

A Prayer for the Promised Rest.

DEAR Friend of friendless sinners, hear,
  And magnify Thy grace Divine;
Pardon a worm that would draw near,
  That would his heart to Thee resign:
A worm, by self and sin opprest,
That pants to reach Thy promised rest.

With holy fear and reverent love,
  I long to lie beneath Thy throne;
I long in Thee to live and move,
  And stay myself on Thee alone:
Teach me to lean upon Thy breast,
To find in Thee the promised Rest.

Thou say'st Thou wilt Thy servants keep
  In perfect peace, whose minds shall be,
Like new-born babes, or helpless sheep,
  Completely stay'd, dear Lord, on Thee:
How calm their state, how truly blest,
Who trust on Thee, the promised Rest!

Take me, my Saviour, as Thine own,
  And vindicate my righteous cause,
Be Thou my portion, Lord, alone,
  And bend me to obey Thy laws:
In Thy dear arms of love caress'd,
Give me to find Thy promised rest!

F

Bid the tempestuous rage of sin,
   With all its wrathful fury, die;
Let the Redeemer dwell within,
   And turn my sorrows into joy:
O may my heart, by Thee possess'd,
Know Thee to be my promised Rest!

                             R. Hill.

Contentment Encouraged.

LET ocean's waves tumultuous rise,
And strive in vain to pierce the skies
   And mingle with the stars;
Then disappointed backward roll,
And, wild with rage, disturb the pole
   With their presumptuous wars.

Let rebel angels, doom'd to fire,
Provoke the dread Eternal's ire
   And combat with their God;
Then headlong from th' ethereal height
Precipitate their downward flight
   At His effective nod.

Let murmuring mortals, too, repine,
Arraign the Providence Divine,
   And blame the deeds of Heaven;
While passions strong, without control,
Disturb the agitated soul,
   Enraged at what is given.

But shall the Christian's nobler mind—
By grace renew'd, by Heaven refined—
   Indulge a murmuring thought?
Shall he who claims Jehovah's strength,
Who shall be brought to heaven at length,
   Bemoan *his* present lot?

Forbid it, gracious God! he cries,
Nor let th' ungenerous thought arise,
   Offspring of discontent!
No! while my God, my Saviour lives,
Thankful I'll take whate'er He gives,
   And prize the blessings sent.

Since He has said, " I'll ne'er depart,"
I'll bind His promise to my heart,
   Rejoicing in His care:
This shall support while here I live;
And, when in glory I arrive,
   I'll praise Him for it there.

                           S. Pearce.

Desiring to Praise God.

ALMIGHTY Author of my frame,
To Thee my vital pow'rs belong;
Thy praise, delightful, glorious theme!
Demands my heart, my life, my tongue.

My heart, my life, my tongue are Thine,
O be Thy praise their bless'd employ!
But may my song with angels join,
Nor sacred awe forbid the joy?

Thy glories the seraphic lyre,
On all its strings, attempts in vain;
Then how shall mortals dare aspire,
In thought, to try th' unequal strain?

Yet the great Sov'reign of the skies
To mortals bends a gracious ear,
Nor the mean tribute will despise,
When offer'd with a heart sincere.

Great God! accept the humble praise,
And guide my heart, and guide my tongue;
While to Thy name I trembling raise
The grateful, though unworthy song.

Steele.

Thanksgiving and Praise.

" My soul, praise the Lord, speak good of His name!"
His mercies record, His bounties proclaim;
To God their Creator let all creatures raise
The song of thanksgiving, the chorus of praise.

Though hid from man's sight, God sits on His throne,
Yet here by His works their Author is known:
The world shines a mirror its Maker to show,
And heav'n views its image reflected below.

By knowledge supreme, by wisdom Divine,
God governs this earth with gracious design :
O'er beast, bird, and insect His Providence reigns,
Whose will first created, whose love still sustains.

And man, His last work, with reason endu'd,
Who, falling through sin, by grace is renew'd ;
To God, his Creator, let man ever raise
The song of thanksgiving, the chorus of praise.

Park.

General Praise.

LET us, with a joyful mind,
Praise the Lord, for He is kind ;
For His mercies shall endure,
Ever faithful, ever sure.

Let us sound His name abroad ;
For of gods He is the God,
Who by wisdom did create
Th' heavens high, and all their state ;

Did the solid earth ordain
How to rise above the main ;
Who, by His commanding might,
Fill'd the new-made world with light ;

Caused the golden-tressèd sun
All the day his course to run ;
And the moon to shine by night,
'Mid her spangled sisters bright.

All His creatures God does feed,
His full hand supplies their need ;
Let us, therefore, warble forth
His high majesty and worth.

He His mansion hath on high,
'Bove the reach of mortal eye ;
And His mercies shall endure,
Ever faithful, ever sure.

Milton.

Praise to God.

BEGIN, my soul, the lofty strain ;
   In solemn accents sing
A sacred hymn of grateful praise
   To heav'n's almighty King.

Ye curling fountains, as you roll
   Your silver waves along,
Whisper to all your verdant shores
   The subject of my song.

Bear it, ye winds, on all your wings,
   To distant climes away,
And round the wide-extended world
   The lofty theme convey.

Take the glad burden of His name,
   Ye clouds, as you arise,
Whether to deck the golden morn,
   Or shade the evening skies.

Praise and Thanksgiving.

Long let it warble round the spheres,
    And echo through the sky :
Let angels, with immortal skill,
    Improve the harmony;

While we, with sacred rapture fired,
    The blest Creator sing,
And chant our consecrated lays
    To heav'n's eternal King.

Mrs. Rowe.

Praise to God through the Whole of our Existence.

God of my life, through all its days
My grateful pow'rs shall sound Thy praise ;
The song shall wake with opening light,
And warble to the silent night.

When anxious cares would break my rest,
And griefs would tear my throbbing breast,
Thy tuneful praises raised on high
Shall check the murmur and the sigh.

When death o'er nature shall prevail,
And all its pow'rs of language fail,
Joy through my swimming eyes shall break,
And mean the thanks I cannot speak.

But, oh, when that last conflict 's o'er,
And I am chain'd to flesh no more,
With what glad accents shall I rise,
To join the music of the skies!

Soon shall I learn th' exalted strains
Which echo o'er the heav'nly plains,
And emulate, with joy unknown,
The glowing seraphs round Thy throne.

The cheerful tribute will I give,
Long as a deathless soul can live ;
A work so sweet, a theme so high,
Demands and crowns eternity.

Doddridge.

Praise for Daily Mercies.

WE'LL proclaim the wondrous story
    Of the mercies we receive,
From the day-spring's dawning glory,
    Till the fading hour of eve.

All the blessings Heav'n is lending
    We'll extol in grateful lays ;
To His radiant throne ascending,
    Wafted on the wings of praise.

In exalted rapture joining,
    We'll employ our happy days,
All our grateful hearts combining
    To declare His endless praise.

Handel.

Praise for Redeeming Love.

Now begin the heav'nly theme,
Sing aloud in Jesus' name :
Ye who His salvation prove,
Triumph in redeeming love.

Ye who see the Father's grace
Beaming in the Saviour's face,
As to Canaan on ye move,
Praise and bless redeeming love.

Mourning souls, dry up your tears,
Banish all your guilty fears ;
See your guilt and curse remove,
Cancell'd by redeeming love.

Ye, alas ! who long have been
Willing slaves of death and sin,
Now from bliss no longer rove,
Stop and taste redeeming love.

Welcome all by sin opprest ;
Welcome to His sacred rest :
Nothing brought Him from above —
Nothing but redeeming love.

He subdued th' infernal pow'rs ;
Those tremendous foes of ours,
From their cursèd empire drove,
Mighty in redeeming love.

Hither, then, your music bring,
Strike aloud each cheerful string ;
Mortals join the host above,
Join to praise redeeming love.

Anon.

Praise for Divine Goodness.

Lift up to God the voice of praise,
  Whose breath our souls inspired;
Loud and more loud the anthems raise,
  With grateful ardour fired !

Lift up to God the voice of praise,
  Whose tender care sustains
Our feeble frame, encompass'd round
  With death's unnumber'd pains.

Lift up to God the voice of praise,
  Whose goodness passeth thought,
Loads ev'ry minute, as it flies,
  With benefits unsought.

Lift up to God the voice of praise,
  From whom salvation flows,
Who sent His Son our souls to save
  From everlasting woes.

Lift up to God the voice of praise,
  For hope's transporting ray,
Which lights, through darkest shades of death,
  To realms of endless day.

Wardlaw's Col.

Affliction.

Doth His Promise Fail?

How sweet on Thy bosom to rest
When nature's affliction is near !
The soul that can trust Thee is blest ;
Thy smile gives deliv'rance from fear.

The Lord has in kindness declared,
That those who will trust in His name
Shall in the sharp conflict be spared,
His mercy and love to proclaim.

This promise shall be to my soul
A messenger sent from the skies,
An anchor when billows shall roll,
A refuge when tempests arise.

O Saviour, Thy promise fulfil,
Its comfort impart to my mind ;
Then calmly I'll bow to Thy will,
To the cup of affliction resign'd.

Anon.

Confidence in God.

THE thoughts of my heart, they are known,
All known to the Guide of my youth :
He never will leave me alone
To question His love or His truth.

Heavenly Melodies.

Till now He has prosper'd my course,
And greatly exceeded my prayer,
And still is the blessed resource
To which I may ever repair.

Our lives and our times are with Him
Who sees from the first to the last.
He raises my cup to the brim,
Or empties my vessel as fast.

His purpose and love are the same,
Whatever the changes I find:
A trifle may alter my frame,
But nothing unsettles His mind.

Reed.

Afflictions Sanctified by the Word.

O now I love Thy holy word,
Thy gracious covenant, O Lord!
It guides me in the peaceful way;
I think upon it all the day.

What are the mines of shining wealth,
The strength of youth, the bloom of health—
What are all joys, compared with those
Thine everlasting word bestows?

Affliction.

Long unafflicted, undismay'd,
In pleasure's path secure I stray'd;
Thou mad'st me feel Thy chast'ning rod,
And straight I turn'd unto my God.

What though it pierced my fainting heart;
I bless Thine hand that caused the smart:
It taught my tears awhile to flow,
But saved me from eternal woe.

Oh! hadst Thou left me unchastised
Thy precept I had still despised;
And still the snare in secret laid
Had my unwary feet betray'd.

I love Thee, therefore, O my God,
And breathe towards Thy dear abode,
Where, in Thy presence, fully blest,
Thy chosen saints for ever rest.

Cowper.

The Sufferer Supported by a Contemplation of the Saviour's Agonies.

He knelt, the Saviour knelt and pray'd,
    When but His Father's eye
Look'd through the lonely garden's shade
    On that dread agony:
The Lord of all above, beneath,
Was bow'd with sorrow unto death!

The sun set in a fearful hour,
  The stars might well grow dim,
When this mortality had power
  So to o'ershadow Him!
That He who gave man's breath might know
The very depths of human woe.

He proved them all; the doubt, the strife,
  The faint, perplexing dread,
The mists that hang o'er parting life,
  All gather'd round His head:
And the Deliverer knelt to pray—
Yet pass'd it not, that cup, away.

It pass'd not—though the stormy wave
  Had sunk beneath His tread;
It pass'd not—though to Him the grave
  Had yielded up its dead:
But there was sent Him from on high
A gift of strength for man to die.

And was the Sinless thus beset
  With anguish and dismay?
How may we meet our conflict yet,
  In death's dark, narrow way?
Through Him—through Him, that path who trod.
Save, or we perish, Son of God!

Hemans.

Divine Mercies and Judgments Compared.

In Thy rebukes, all-gracious God,
　What soft compassion reigns !
What gentle accents of Thy voice
　Assuage Thy children's pains !

My Father, God : how sweet the sound,
　How tender, and how dear !
Not all the melody of heav'n
　Could so delight the ear.

Come, sacred Spirit, seal the name
　On mine expanding heart,
And show that in Jehovah's grace
　I share a filial part.

Cheer'd by a signal so Divine,
　Unwav'ring, I believe :
Thou know'st I Abba, Father, cry,
　Nor can the sign deceive.

On wings of everlasting love
　The Comforter is come ;
All terrors at his voice disperse,
　And endless pleasures bloom.

Doddridge.

God bringing His People into the Covenant under the Rod.

How gracious and how wise
Is our chastising God!
And, oh, how rich the blessings are
Which blossom from His rod!

He lifts it up on high,
With pity in His heart,
That ev'ry stroke His children feel
May grace and peace impart.

Instructed thus, they bow,
And own His sov'reign sway;
They turn their erring footsteps back
To His forsaken way.

His cov'nant love they seek,
And seek the happy bands
That closer still engage their hearts
To honour His commands.

Dear Father, we consent
To discipline Divine,
And bless the pains that make our souls
Still more completely Thine.

Doddridge.

Why art thou Cast down?

BE still, my heart! these anxious cares
To thee are burdens, thorns, and snares;
They cast dishonour on thy Lord,
And contradict His gracious word!

Brought safely by His hand thus far,
Why wilt thou now give place to fear?
How canst thou want if He provide,
Or lose thy way with such a Guide?

When first, before His mercy-seat,
Thou didst to Him thy all commit,
He gave thee warrant, from that hour,
To trust His wisdom, love, and pow'r.

Did ever trouble yet befall,
And He refuse to hear thy call?
And has He not His promise past
That thou shalt overcome at last?

He who has help'd me hitherto
Will help me all my journey through,
And give me daily cause to raise
New Ebenezers to His praise.

Though rough and thorny be the road,
It leads thee home, apace, to God;
Then count thy present trials small,
For heav'n will make amends for all.

Newton.

G

Christ's Pity, etc., for His Disciples.

PEACE, all ye sorrows of the heart;
  And all my tears, be dry:
That Christian ne'er can be forlorn
  That views his Jesus nigh.

" Let not your bosoms throb," He says,
  "Nor be your souls afraid!
Trust in your God's almighty name,
  And trust your Saviour's aid.

" Fair mansions in My Father's house
  For all His children wait;
And I, your Elder Brother, go,
  To open wide the gate.

" And, if I thither go before,
  A dwelling to prepare,
I surely shall return again,
  That I may fix you there.

" United in eternal love
  My chosen shall remain,
And with rejoicing hearts shall share
  The honours of My reign."

Yes, Lord, Thy gracious words we hear,
  And cordial joys they bring:
Frail nature may extort a groan,
  But faith shall learn to sing.

Doddridge.

The Comforts of Religion.

When gloomy thoughts and boding fears
   The trembling heart invade,
And all the face of nature wears
   An universal shade,

Religion's dictates can assuage
   The tempest of the soul,
And ev'ry storm shall cease to rage
   At her Divine control.

Through life's bewilder'd, darksome way,
   Her hand, unerring, leads,
And o'er the path her heav'nly ray
   A cheering lustre sheds.

When feeble reason, tired and blind,
   Sinks helpless and afraid,
Thou blest supporter of the mind,
   How pow'rful is Thine aid!

O let my heart confess Thy pow'r,
   And find Thy sweet relief,
To brighten ev'ry gloomy hour,
   And soften ev'ry grief.

Steele.

Humble Reliance upon God.

My God, my Father, blissful name!
   O may I call Thee mine?
May I with sweet assurance claim
   A portion so Divine?

This only can my fears control,
  And bid my sorrows fly :
What harm can ever reach my soul
  Beneath my Father's eye ?

Whate'er thy providence denies
  I calmly would resign ;
For Thou art good, and just, and wise :
  O bend my will to Thine.

Whate'er Thy sacred will ordains,
  O give me strength to bear ;
And let me know my Father reigns,
  And trust His tender care.

If pain and sickness rend this frame,
  And life almost depart,
Is not Thy mercy still the same
  To cheer my drooping heart ?

Thy sov'reign ways are all unknown
  To my weak, erring sight ;
Yet let my soul, adoring, own
  That all Thy ways are right.

My God, my Father, be Thy name
  My solace and my stay :
O wilt Thou seal my humble claim,
  And drive my fears away ?

Steele.

Christian Courage, Fortitude, and Hope.

Come on, my partners in distress,
My comrades through the wilderness,
  Who still your bodies feel,
Awhile forget your griefs and fears,
And look beyond the vale of tears
  To that celestial hill.

Beyond the bounds of time and space,
Look forward to that happy place,
  The saints' secure abode ;
On faith's strong eagle-pinions rise,
And force your passage to the skies,
  And scale the mount of God.

See where the Lamb in glory stands,
Encircled with His radiant bands,
  And join th' angelic pow'rs ;
For all that height of glorious bliss
Our everlasting portion is,
  And all that heav'n is ours.

Who suffer for our Master here,
We shall before His face appear,
  And by His side sit down:
To patient faith the prize is sure,
And all that to the end endure
  The cross shall wear the crown.

Thrice blessèd bliss-inspiring hope !
It lifts the fainting spirits up ;
   It brings to life the dead :
Our conflicts here shall soon be past,
And you and I ascend at last
   Triumphant with our Head.

C. Wesley.

A Fountain shall come forth of the House of the Lord.

Jesus ! how heavenly is the place
Where Thine own servants wait for Thee ;
Where the rich fountain of Thy grace
Stands ever open, full and free !

Hungry, and poor, and lame, and blind,
Hither Thy ransom'd people fly ;
In Thy deep wounds a balsam find,
And live while they behold Thee die.

Here they forget their doubts and fears,
While Thy sharp sorrows meet their eyes ;
And bless the hand which dries their tears,
And each returning want supplies.

How vast the mysteries of Thy love !
How high, how wide, how deep it rolls !
Its fountain-springs in heaven above ;
Its streams revive our drooping souls.

Anon.

The Ways of Wisdom Pleasant.

How happy is the man who hears
    Instruction's warning voice,
And who celestial wisdom makes
    His early, only choice !

Wisdom has treasures greater far
    Than east or west unfold,
And her rewards more precious are
    Than is the gain of gold.

In her right hand she holds to view
    A length of happy years,
And in her left the prize of fame
    And honour bright appears.

She guides the young with innocence,
    In pleasure's path to tread :
A crown of glory she bestows
    Upon the hoary head.

According as her labours rise,
    So her rewards increase ;
Her ways are ways of pleasantness,
    And all her paths are peace.

Logan.

Religion the Road to Happiness.

O HAPPINESS, thou pleasing dream,
    Where is thy substance found ?
Sought through the varying scenes in vain
    Through earth's capacious round.

Religion's sacred lamp alone,
   Unerring, points the way
Where happiness for ever shines
   With unpolluted ray;

To regions of eternal peace,
   Beyond the starry skies,
Where pure, sublime, and perfect joys
   In endless prospect rise.

Anon.

Praise for a Good Hope.

THANKS to my God for every gift
   His bounteous hands bestow,
And thanks eternal for that love
   Whence all those comforts flow.

For ever let my grateful heart
   His boundless grace adore,
Which gives ten thousand blessings now,
   And bids me hope for more.

Transporting hope! still on my soul
   Let thy sweet glories shine,
Till thou thyself art lost in joys
   Immortal and Divine.

Heginbothom.

Blessed State.

Exalted high at God's right hand,
Nearer the throne than cherubs stand,
With glory crown'd, in white array,
My wondering soul says, Who are they?

These are the saints beloved of God:
Wash'd are their robes in Jesus' blood;
More spotless than the purest white,
They shine in uncreated light.

Brighter than angels, lo! they shine,
Their glories great, and all Divine:
Tell me their origin, and say,
Their order what, and whence came they?

Through tribulation great they came;
They bore the cross, and scorn'd the shame:
Within the Living Temple blest,
In God they dwell, and on Him rest.

And does the cross thus prove their gain?
And shall they thus for ever reign,
Seated on sapphire thrones, to praise
The wonders of redeeming grace?

Hunger they ne'er shall feel again,
Nor burning thirst shall they sustain;
To wells of living water led,
By God the Lamb for ever fed.

Unknown to mortal ears, they sing
The secret glories of their King:
Tell me the subject of their lays,
And whence their loud, exalted praise?

Jesus, the Saviour, is their theme;
They sing the wonders of His name;
To Him ascribing power and grace,
Dominion, and eternal praise.

Amen! they cry, to Him alone,
Who dares to fill His Father's throne;
They give Him glory, and again
Repeat His praise, and say, Amen!

Rowland Hill.

Longing for Heaven.

O HAD I the wings of a dove,
I'd make my escape and be gone;
I'd mix with the spirits above,
Who encompass yon heavenly throne;

I'd fly from all labour and toil
To the place where the weary have rest:
I'd haste from contention and broil
To the peaceful abode of the blest.

How happy are they who no more
Have to fear the assaults of the foe!
Arrived on the heavenly shore,
They have left all their conflicts below.

Around that magnificent throne
Where the Lamb all His glory displays,
United for ever in one,
His people are singing His praise.

But no; my desire is not good;
Impatience, not faith, is its source;
While He who redeem'd me with blood
Still says to me, " Carry the cross."

Ah, Lord, let me think of the day
When Thou wast " rejected of men."
And put the base wish far away,
And never be fearful again.

Anon.

Repent.

VAIN man, thy fond pursuits forbear;
　　Repent: thy end is nigh!
Death, at the farthest, is not far:
　　O think before you die!

Reflect: thou hast a soul to save;
　　Thy sins, how high they mount!
What are thy hopes beyond the grave?
　　How stands that dread account?

Death enters, and there's no defence;
　　His time there's none can tell:
He'll in a moment call thee hence,
　　To heaven—or to hell!

Thy body, now thy chiefest care,
  Corruption shall consume ;
But, ah, destruction stops not there !
  Sin kills beyond the tomb !

To-day the Gospel calls : to-day,
  Sinner ! it speaks to you !
Repent—believe—at its command,
  And life and heaven pursue !

Hart.

" So shall we Ever be," etc.

For ever to behold Him shine,
For evermore to call Him mine,
  And see Him still before me ;
For ever on His face to gaze,
And meet His full assembled rays,
While all the Father He displays
  To all the saints in glory !

Not all things else are half so dear
As His delightful presence here :
  What must it be in heaven !
'Tis heaven on earth to hear Him say,
As now I journey day by day,
" Poor sinner, cast thy fears away :
  Thy sins are all forgiven."

But how must His celestial voice
Make my enraptured heart rejoice
  When I in glory hear Him !
While I before the heavenly gate
For everlasting entrance wait,
And Jesus on His throne of state
  Invites me to come near Him !

"Come in, thou blessèd, sit by Me ;
With My own life I ransom'd thee ;
  Come, taste My perfect favour :
Come in, thou happy spirit, come :
Thou now shalt dwell with Me at home ;
Ye blissful mansions, make him room,
  For he must stay for ever."

Anon.

Looking Forward.

From every earthly pleasure,
  From every transient joy,
From every mortal treasure
  That soon will fade and die ;
No longer these desiring,
  Upwards our wishes tend,
To nobler bliss aspiring,
  And joys that never end.

From every piercing sorrow
  That heaves our breast to-day,
Or threatens us to-morrow,
  Hope turns our eyes away;
On wings of faith ascending,
  We see the land of light,
And feel our sorrows ending
  In infinite delight.

'Tis true we are but strangers
  And sojourners below,
And countless snares and dangers
  Surround the path we go:
Though painful and distressing,
  Yet there's a rest above;
And onward still we're pressing,
  To reach that land of love.

Anon.

They Ascended up to Heaven.

WHAT a glorious destination,
  Christians, will be yours at last,
When the waves of tribulation,
  Breaking o'er your souls, have past,
    And, triumphant,
Ye shall hear the signal blast!

Heaven.

O look up! 'mid coming danger
   Christ will never let you fall;
He who bought you is no stranger;
   Christ will prove your All-in-all!
      Everlasting
  Is your strong "munition wall."

As Elijah's car of glory,
   Hov'ring o'er a world of woe,
Snatch'd him, with contention weary,
   From the fierce inveterate foe,
      All resplendent
  With the beams of heaven's own glow;

So, 'mid enemies victorious,
   When last hopes of aid shall end,
Will Christ's witnesses, "all glorious,"
   In a cloud to heaven ascend,
      And for ever
  Dwell with Him, their King, their Friend.

                 Anon.

Meetness for Heaven.

Heaven is a place of rest from sin;
But all who hope to enter there
Must here that holy course begin
Which shall their souls for rest prepare.

Clean hearts, O God, in us create;
Right spirits, Lord, in us renew:
Commence we now that higher state,
Now do Thy will as angels do.

A life in heaven! O what is this?
The sum of all that faith believed;
Fulness of joy, and depths of bliss,
Unseen, unfathom'd, unconceived.

While thrones, dominions, princedoms, powers,
And saints, made perfect, triumph thus,
A goodly heritage is ours—
There is a heaven on earth for us.

The church of Christ, the school of grace,
The Spirit teaching by the word!
In those our Saviour's steps we trace:
By this His living voice is heard.

Firm in His footsteps may we tread,
Learn every lesson of His love;
And be from grace to glory led,
From heaven below to heaven above!

Montgomery.

Happiness Approaching.

Awake, ye saints, and raise your eyes,
And raise your voices high;
Awake, and praise that sovereign love
That shows salvation nigh.

On all the wings of time it flies;
   Each moment brings it near:
Then welcome each declining day,
   And each revolving year!

Not many years their rounds shall run,
   Nor many mornings rise,
Ere all its glories stand reveal'd
   To our admiring eyes.

Ye wheels of nature, speed your course!
   Ye mortal powers, decay!
Fast as ye bring the night of death,
   Ye bring eternal day.

                           Doddridge.

The Year of Release is at Hand.

The year of release is at hand:
   What rapture the thought should convey!
To Canaan's fair, beautiful land,
   Sweet angels, come, bear me away.

O why must I lingering stay
   Where no satisfaction I find?
Had I wings, I would hasten away,
   And leave all that's mortal behind.

Confined like a bird to its cage,
   My soul would fain rise on the wing:
I long with the saints to engage
   In a concert of praise to my King.

The year of release is at hand :
   Why should I of troubles complain ?
Adieu : in the promisèd land
   You never shall vex me again.

The bondage of sin there is o'er ;
   The fury of Satan shall cease ;
The world shall perplex me no more :
   O hasten the year of release !

But who this release can convey
   To bondmen and slaves such as we ?
Gethsemane, Calvary, say,
   "'Tis Jesus, who died on the tree."

Then help us to wait for the day,
   And each in his duty to stand ;
But whisper, sweet Spirit, and say,
   "The year of release is at hand."

Anon.

The Weary be at Rest.

When the world my heart is rending
   With its heaviest storms of care,
My glad thoughts, to God ascending,
   Find a refuge from despair.

There's a hand of mercy near me,
   Though the waves of trouble roar ;
There's an hour of rest to cheer me
   When the toils of life are o'er.

Happy hour! when saints are gaining
  That bright crown they long'd to wear;
Not one spot of sin remaining,
  Not one pang of earthly care.

O to rest in peace for ever,
  Join'd with happy souls above,
Where no foe my heart can sever
  From the Saviour whom I love!

This the hope that shall sustain me
  Till life's pilgrimage be past:
Fears may vex, and troubles pain me:
  I shall reach my home at last.

Anon.

The Worship of Heaven.

O FOR a sweet, inspiring ray,
To animate our feeble strains,
From the bright realms of endless day,
The blissful realms where Jesus reigns.

There, low before His glorious throne,
Adoring saints and angels fall,
And, with delightful worship, own
His smile their bliss, their heav'n, their all.

Immortal glories crown His head;
While tuneful hallelujahs rise,
And love, and joy, and triumph spread
Through all th' assemblies of the skies.

He smiles, and seraphs tune their songs
To boundless rapture while they gaze;
Ten thousand thousand joyful tongues
Resound His everlasting praise.

There all the fav'rites of the Lamb
Shall join at last the heavenly choir.
O may the joy-inspiring theme
Awake our faith and warm desire!

Dear Saviour, let Thy Spirit seal
Our interest in that blissful place,
Till death remove this mortal veil,
And we behold Thy lovely face.

Steele.

𝕿𝖍𝖊 𝕭𝖑𝖎𝖘𝖘𝖋𝖚𝖑 𝕾𝖔𝖈𝖎𝖊𝖙𝖞 𝕬𝖇𝖔𝖛𝖊.

How bright is the prospect the saint has in view,
　Let present things be as they may:
Omnipotent mercy shall bring him quite through,
　And guide him to regions of day.

Alas! sin and sorrow attend him while here,
　And frequently injure his peace;
But faith beholds now the sweet season as near
　That brings him a final release.

With rapture he'll mount his celestial abode,
　His spirit find pleasure and rest;
With ecstasy bask in the smiles of his God,
　Partaking the joys of the blest.

With patriarchs, prophets, apostles, and those
  Who seal'd the truth with their blood,
Whose unsubdued courage astonish'd their foes,
  And forced them to glorify God :

United with these, he shall hear them relate
  The tale of their sufferings below ;
The conflicts and toils of their militant state,
  How grace had supported them through.

When this having heard, he rehearses to them
  The mazes through which he has trod ;
From great tribulation by grace how he came,
  And reach'd the fair city of God.

Now all strike their harps, and one chorus they raise ;
  Salvation by grace is their theme ;
Thanksgiving, and honour, and blessing, and praise,
  And glory to God and the Lamb.

Fountain.

The Redeemed in Heaven.

Who are these array'd in white,
  Brighter than the noon-day sun,
Foremost of the sons of light,
  Nearest the eternal throne ?

These are they who bore the cross,
  Faithful to their Master died,
Suffer'd in His righteous cause,
  Followers of the Crucified.

Out of great distress they came,
    And their robes, by faith below,
In the blood of Christ the Lamb
    They have wash'd as white as snow.

More than conquerors at last,
    Here they find their trials o'er :
They have all their suff'rings passed,
    Hunger now and thirst no more.

He that on the throne doth reign
    Them for evermore shall feed,
With the tree of life sustain,
    To the living fountains lead.

He shall all their griefs remove ;
    He shall all their wants supply :
God Himself, the God of love,
    Tears shall wipe from every eye.

De Courcy.

The Heavenly Jerusalem.

High in yonder realms of light,
    Far above these lower skies,
Fair and exquisitely bright,
    Heaven's unfading mansions rise.
Glad within these blest abodes
    Dwell the raptured saints above,
Where no anxious care corrodes,
    Happy in Immanuel's love.

Once, indeed, like us below,
  Pilgrims in this vale of tears,
Torturing pain and heavy woe,
  Gloomy doubts, distressing fears—
These, alas! full well they knew,
  Sad companions of their way;
Oft on them the tempest blew
  Through the long and cheerless day.

Oft their vileness they deplored,
  Wills perverse and hearts untrue,
Grieved they had not loved the Lord,
  Loved, as they had wish'd to do;
But, these days of weeping o'er,
  Past this scene of toil and pain,
They shall feel distress no more,
  Never, never weep again.

Happy spirits, ye are fled
  Where no grief can entrance find;
Lull'd to rest the aching head,
  Soothed the anguish of the mind.
Every tear is wiped away;
  Sighs no more shall heave the breast;
Night is lost in endless day,
  Sorrow in eternal rest.

Raffles.

Death Overcome.

Ye saints, who once languish'd below,
   But long since have enter'd your rest,
I pant to be glorified too,
   To lean on Immanuel's breast.
The grave in which Jesus was laid
   Has buried my guilt and my fears,
And while I contemplate its shade,
   The light of His presence appears.

O sweet is the season of rest,
   When life's weary journey is done—
The blush that spreads over its west;
   The last lingering ray of its sun.
Though dreary the empire of night,
   I soon shall emerge from its gloom,
And see immortality's light
   Arise on the shades of the tomb.

Then welcome the last rending sighs,
   When these aching heart-strings shall break,
When death shall extinguish these eyes,
   And moisten with dew this pale cheek:
No terror the prospect begets;
   I am not mortality's slave;
The sunbeam of life as it sets
   Paints a rainbow of peace on the grave.

                                        Collyer.

Happiness of Departed Believers.

How happy are the souls above,
   From sin and sorrow free !
With Jesus they are now at rest,
   And all His glory see.

" Worthy the Lamb !" aloud they cry,
   " That brought us here to God :"
In ceaseless hymns of praise they shout
   The merit of His blood.

With wondering joy they recollect
   Their fears and dangers past ;
And bless the wisdom, power, and love
   Which brought them safe at last.

They follow the exalted Lamb
   Where'er they see Him go ;
And at the footstool of His grace
   Their blood-bought crowns they throw.

Lord, let the merit of Thy death
   To me be likewise given ;
And I, with them, will shout Thy praise
   Through all the courts of heaven.

Toplady.

The Everlasting Song.

EARTH has engross'd my love too long:
   'Tis time I lift mine eyes
Upward, dear Father, to Thy throne,
   And to my native skies.

There the blest Man, my Saviour, sits:
   The God! how bright He shines!
And scatters infinite delights
   On all the happy minds.

Seraphs with elevated strains
   Circle the throne around,
And move and charm the starry plains
   With an immortal sound.

Jesus, the Lord, their harps employs:
   Jesus, my love, they sing!
Jesus, the life of both our joys,
   Sounds sweet from every string.

Hark, how beyond the narrow bound
   Of time and space they run,
And echo in majestic sounds
   The Godhead of the Son.

And now they sink the lofty tune,
   And gentler notes they play;
And bring the Father's Equal down,
   To dwell in humble clay.

O sacred beauties of the Man!
  (The God resides within):
His flesh all pure, without a stain;
  His soul without a sin.

But, when to Calvary they turn,
  Silent their harps abide;
Suspended songs, a moment mourn
  The God that loved and died.

Then, all at once, to living strains
  They summon every chord,
Tell how He triumph'd o'er His pains,
  And chant the rising Lord.

Now let me mount and join their song,
  And be an angel too:
My heart, my ear, my hand, my tongue,
  Here's joyful work for you.

I would begin the music here,
  And so my soul should rise:
O for some heavenly notes to bear
  My passions to the skies!

There ye that love my Saviour sit:
  There I would fain have place,
Among your thrones or at your feet,
  So I might see His face.

Anon.

The Redeemed.

I saw, and lo! a countless throng,
Th' elect of every nation, name, and tongue,
Assembled round the everlasting throne;
    With robes of white endued,
    The righteousness of God;
    And each a palm sustain'd
    In his victorious hand;
When thus the bright, melodious choir begun:
    " Salvation to Thy name,
Eternal God, and co-eternal Lamb!
In power, in glory, and in essence one!"

So sung the saints. Th' angelic train
Second the anthem with a loud Amen
    (These in the outer circle stood:
    The saints were nearest God);
And prostrate fall, with glory overpower'd,
    And hide their faces with their wings,
    And thus address the King of kings:
" All hail! by Thy triumphant Church adored!
    Blessing and thanks and honour too
Are Thy supreme, Thy everlasting due,
Our Triune Sovereign, our propitious Lord!"

While I beheld th' amazing sight,
A seraph pointed to the saints in white,
And told me who they were, and whence they came:

"These are they whose lot below
Was persecution, pain, and woe ;
These are the chosen, purchased flock,
Who ne'er their Lord forsook ;
Through His imputed merit free from blame ;
Redeem'd from every sin ;
And, as thou seest, whose garments were made clean,
Wash'd in the blood of yon exalted Lamb.

" Saved by His righteousness alone,
Spotless they stand before the throne,
And in th' ethereal temple chant His praise :
Himself among them deigns to dwell,
And face to face His light reveal :
Hunger and thirst, as heretofore,
And pain, and heat, they know no more,
Nor need, as once, the sun's prolific rays :
Immanuel here His people feeds,
To streams of joy perennial leads,
And wipes, for ever wipes, the tears from every face."

Happy the souls released from fear,
And safely landed there !
Some of the shining number once I knew,
And travell'd with them here :
Nay, some, my elder brethren now,
Set later out for heaven, my junior saints below :
Long after me they heard the call of grace
Which waked them unto righteousness :
How have they got beyond ?

Converted last, yet first with glory crown'd!
  Little, once, I thought that these
    Would first the summit gain,
And leave me far behind, slow journeying through the
    plain.

Loved while on earth! nor less beloved though gone!
  Think not I envy you your crown:
No! if I could, I would not call you down!
    Though slower is my pace,
    To you I'll follow on,
  Leaning on Jesus all the way;
  Who, now and then, lets fall a ray
    Of comfort from His throne:
    The shinings of His grace
Soften my passage through the wilderness;
And vines, nectareous, spring where briers grew:
  The sweet unveilings of His face
Make me, at times, near half as blest as you!
O might His beauty feast my ravish'd eyes!
  His gladdening presence ever stay,
  And cheer me all my journey through!
But soon the clouds return; my triumph dies;
  Damp vapours from the valley rise,
And hide the hill of Sion from my view.

  Spirit of Light! thrice holy Dove!
Brighten my sense of interest in that love
Which knew no birth, and never shall expire.

Electing Goodness, firm and free,
My whole salvation hangs on thee,
Eldest and fairest daughter of Eternity!
Redemption, grace, and glory too,
Our bliss above, and hopes below,
From her, their parent-fountain, flow.
Ah! tell me, Lord, that Thou hast chosen me!
Thou, who hast kindled my intense desire,
Fulfil the wish Thy influence did inspire,
And let me my election know!
Then, when Thy summons bids me come up higher,
Well pleased I shall from life retire,
And join the burning hosts, beheld at distance now.

Augustus Montague Toplady.

Lines Composed on the Death of a Clergyman's Little Girl.

I've lost my little girl at last,
The loving father cried:
The sweetest babe I ever saw
Is taken from my side.

I fondly hoped to have saved her life,
Again to have seen her play,
And heard her little prattling voice:
Alas! she's gone away.

I laid her in a sylvan grave,
   A green and soft retreat.
The sweetest flowers I planted there,
   The lily at her feet.

The violets, daisies, evergreens,
   Are close beside her too.
Her grave with many flowers I strew :
   'Tis all that I can do.

I sometimes think it's all a dream,
   And say I hear her song ;
I start to clasp my child once more,
   And happiest feelings throng :

A moment more no sounds are heard,
   My fancies all are fled :
The little voice is very still ;
   It's number'd with the dead.

I fancy now I oft can see
   Her sweet, enchanting smile,
As folded in my arms she'd lie,
   And softly sleep awhile.

I wish that she were back again,
   In all her childish glee :
My hope, my joy, my darling babe,
   With thee I long to be.

I sit within my quiet room,
  And think for hours there;
I miss my little one so much,
  And grieve, though not despair.

I miss her with her toys at play
  In silence by my side;
I miss her everywhere all day:
  Can she be gone to hide?

O, no; she has for ever sped
  Upward her rapid flight,
To be for ever, evermore,
  Array'd in spotless white.

Sweetly and safely now she rests:
  O do not grieve or weep!
Dry up those bitter falling tears:
  She's gently hush'd to sleep.

My Father, help me now to say,
  Most holy is Thy will;
Grant me submission day by day,
  And whisper, Peace, be still.

Henry Jennings.

Thy Will be Done!

My God and Father, while I stray
Far from my home, on life's rough way.
O teach me from my heart to say,
  Thy will be done!

Though dark my path and sad my lot,
Let me be still and murmur not,
Or breathe the prayer divinely taught,
    Thy will be done!

What though in lonely grief I sigh
For friends beloved, no longer nigh,
Submissive still would I reply,
    Thy will be done!

Though Thou hast call'd me to resign
What most I prized, it ne'er was mine;
I have but yielded what was Thine:
    Thy will be done!

Should grief or sickness waste away
My life in premature decay,
My Father! still I strive to say,
    Thy will be done.

Let but my fainting heart be blest
With Thy sweet Spirit for its guest,
My God, to Thee I leave the rest:
    Thy will be done!

Renew my will from day to day;
Blend it with Thine; and take away
All that now makes it hard to say,
    Thy will be done!

Then, when on earth I breathe no more
The prayer, oft mix'd with tears before,
I'll sing upon a happier shore,
    Thy will be done!   *Charlotte Elliott.*

𝔗he 𝔅lank.

THE flowers of Spring have come and gone :
  Bright were the blossoms, brief their stay ;
They shone, and they were shone upon ;
  They flourish'd, faded, pass'd away.
So, hidden from our sorrowing eyes,
Our young, sweet spring-bloom buried lies :
One blast of earth swept o'er the flower ;
It died, the blossom of an hour.

The Summer flowers are freshly blowing
  Beneath glad July's genial morn ;
Like smiles the face of earth bestrowing,
  For fragrance and for beauty born.
My summer-flower has pass'd away :
'Tis now a blank where all was gay—
A blank where, at each evening's close,
I hoped to watch my budding rose.

Soon Autumn, with o'erflowing measure,
  Will hang, upon each bending tree,
The clusters of its golden treasure,
  The life of earth's vast family.
Alas, in one disastrous hour,
From my green vine has fall'n the flower !
A blighted hue its branches wear ;
My autumn-tree looks cold and bare.

And Winter, with its blast wide-roaming,
   In cloud and darkness shall come forth,
Beneath its grave of snow entombing
   The varied verdure of the earth.
But my sweet blossom, safely laid,
Beneath yon cloister's solemn shade,
In gentle, undisturb'd repose,
Shall sleep in winter's grave of snows.

Horatius Bonar.

Life's Changes.

When I survey life's varied scene,
   Amid the darkest hours
Sweet rays of comfort shine between,
   And thorns are mix'd with flowers.

Lord, teach me to adore Thy hand,
   From whence my comforts flow,
And let me in this desert land
   A glimpse of Canaan know.

And O! whate'er of earthly bliss
   Thy sovereign hand denies,
Accepted at Thy throne of grace
   Let this petition rise:

Give me a calm, a thankful heart,
   From every murmur free;
The blessings of Thy grace impart,
   And let me live to Thee.

Let the sweet hope that Thou art mine
  My path of life attend,
Thy presence through my journey shine,
  And bless its happy end!   '

                     Steele.

Trust and Confidence.

Away, my unbelieving fears!
Let fear in me no more take place.
My Saviour doth not yet appear;
He hides the brightness of His face:
But shall I therefore let Him go,
And basely to the tempter yield?
No; in the strength of Jesus, no!
I never will give up my shield!

Although the vine its fruit deny,
Although the olive yield no oil,
The withering fig-tree droop and die,
The field illude the tiller's toil,
The empty stall no herd afford,
And perish all the bleating race,
Yet will I triumph in the Lord!
The God of my salvation praise!

Away, each unbelieving fear!
Let fear to cheering hope give place:
My Saviour will at length appear,
And show the brightness of His face.

Though now my prospects all be cross'd,
My blooming hopes cut off I see,
Still will I in my Jesus trust,
Whose boundless love can reach to me.

In hope—believing against hope—
His promised mercy will I claim;
His gracious word shall bear me up
To seek salvation in His name:
Soon, my dear Saviour, bring it nigh:
My soul shall then outstrip the wind,
On wings of love mount up on high,
And leave the world and sin behind.

Anon.

Kindred Affection.

TWENTY-NINE years have flown since we
Were filled with the purest joy
At first to hear and then to see
Our sweet and pretty baby-boy,
Whose birth made sacred joy to gush,
And drew the true heart's warmest tear,
As the most loving voice cried, Hush!
Sleep, darling babe; sleep sweetly, dear,

Your childish days we oft recall,
When we, with fond parental joy,
Bold at the throne of grace did fall,
And there present our lovely boy.

Of by-gone hours we often tell,
When you were happy with us here :
We hope again to meet and dwell
On Britain's shores, to all most dear.

Our love is still as strong, the same,
Though we are parted for awhile,
As when the little stranger came,
To cheer with childish laugh and smile.
Once more we hail your natal day,
And parents, brother, sister, all
For you will praise, for you will pray,
And for the best of blessings call.

Receive our cordial greetings now,
Our hearts' most pure and fondest love ;
And may we meet once more to bow
Here in our happy home of love.
But, if we ne'er should meet again,
O let us seek to meet above,
Where there's no parting, care, or pain,
But all is joy, and peace, and love.

Farewell, dear boy, for a season—
When we shall meet we cannot tell ;
That outstrips the guess of reason,
And that we leave to God—farewell.
Soon may we change the word *farewell*,
And all welcome you back once more,
To live with us, and long to dwell
On this thy native island shore.

                                   Henry Jennings.

Trust, and be not Afraid.

BEGONE, unbelief! my Saviour is near,
And for my relief will surely appear :
By prayer let me wrestle, and He will perform;
With Christ in the vessel, I smile at the storm.

Though dark be my way, since He is my guide,
'Tis mine to obey, 'tis His to provide :
Though cisterns be broken, and creatures all fail,
The word He has spoken shall surely prevail.

His love in time past forbids me to think
He'll leave me at last in trouble to sink :
Each sweet Ebenezer I have in review
Confirms His good pleasure to help me quite through.

Determined to save, He watch'd o'er my path
When, Satan's blind slave, I sported with death ;
And can He have taught me to trust in His name,
And thus far have brought me, to put me to shame ?

Why should I complain of want or distress,
Temptation or pain ? He told me no less ;
The heirs of salvation, I know from His word,
Through much tribulation must follow their Lord.

How bitter that cup no heart can conceive,
Which He drank quite up, that sinners might live !
His way was much rougher and darker than mine :
Did Christ, my Lord, suffer, and shall I repine ?

Since all that I meet shall work for my good,
The bitter is sweet, the med'cine is food;
Though painful at present, 'twill cease before long,
And then O how pleasant the conqueror's song!

Newton.

Songs in the Night.

The shades of the ev'ning had closed over all,
And sweet sleep had fallen on cottage and hall;
The night had thrown o'er earth her mantle of gloom,
And only the night-loving flowers could bloom.

I wander'd alone 'neath the star-lighted sky.
Those bright orbs of glory look'd down from on high,
Like angels in heaven, as watchers who stand,
And guard this fair world with their lamps in their hand.

My heart was oppress'd with the day's noise and care,
For troubles like billows had come to me there;
And thoughts rose of murm'ring, as softly I stept,
While round me all nature so peacefully slept;

When sudden a sweet song there fell on my ear,
A nightingale's melody, joyous and clear:
It seem'd that 'mid darkness the bird could not rest,
But sent up its praise-notes to yon home so blest.

And methought, as I listen'd, the song seem'd to bring
Glad thoughts to my heart of yon glorious King,
Whose love can make even the darkness seem light,
And gives to the weary ones " songs in the night."

Katie.

Shadows on the Pathway.

THE everchanging shadows,
  How beautiful they gleam,
If dancing on our pathway,
  Or flick'ring down the stream!
Sometimes the glad reflection
  Of green trees' quiet grace
Fills our spirits with sweet pleasure
  In many a country place.

The sunlight sometimes gleams down
  With rays of garish light:
If 'twere not for the shadows,
  It would be all *too* bright.
Our eyes are weak and trembling:
  They cannot bear for long
The rays of light, so dazzling,
  So brilliant, and so strong.

We learn in many a lesson
  The gladness of the thought,
When we can bear all sunlight
  No shadows will be brought;
But, in this busy world of ours,
  Which we have daily trod,
'Tis the shadows on the pathway
  That lead our souls to God!

Katie.

𝔗𝔥𝔢 𝔘𝔰𝔢𝔣𝔲𝔩 𝔏𝔦𝔣𝔢.

Go, labour on ; spend, and be spent—
   Thy joy to do the Father's will.
It is the way the Master went :
   Should not the servant tread it still ?

Go, labour on ; 'tis not for nought :
   Thy earthly loss is heavenly gain.
Men heed thee, love thee, praise thee not.
   The Master praises : what are men ?

Go, labour on : enough, while here,
   If He shall praise thee, if He deign
Thy willing heart to mark and cheer.
   No toil for Him shall be in vain.

Go, labour on : your hands are weak,
   Your knees are faint, your soul cast down ;
Yet falter not; the prize you seek
   Is near—a kingdom and a crown.

Go, labour on while it is day :
   The world's dark night is hastening on.
Speed, speed thy work; cast sloth away :
   It is not thus that souls are won.

Men die in darkness at your side,
   Without a hope to cheer the tomb :
Take up the torch, and wave it wide,
   The torch that lights time's thickest gloom.

Toil on, faint not, keep watch and pray ;
    Be wise the erring soul to win ;
Go forth into the world's highway ;
    Compel the wand'rer to come in.

Toil on, and in thy toil rejoice ;
    For toil comes rest, for exile home :
Soon shalt thou hear the Bridegroom's voice,
    The midnight peal, Behold, I come !

Horatius Bonar.

Well with the Righteous.

What cheering words are these !
    Their sweetness who can tell ?
In time and in eternity
    'Tis with the righteous well.

'Tis well when joys arise,
    'Tis well when sorrows flow,
'Tis well when darkness veils the skies,
    And strong temptations blow.

'Tis well when, on the mount,
    They feast on dying love ;
And 'tis as well, in God's account,
    When they the furnace prove.

'Tis well when, at His throne,
    They wrestle, weep, and pray :
'Tis well when, at His feet, they groan,
    Yet bring their wants away.

'Tis well when Jesus calls,
" From earth and sin arise :
Join with the host of virgin souls
Made to salvation wise."

Anon.

Haste, Traveller, Haste!

HASTE, traveller, haste ! the night comes on,
And many a shining hour is gone ;
The storm is gathering in the west,
And thou art far from home and rest :
Haste, traveller, haste !

O far from home thy footsteps stray ;
Christ is the Life, and Christ the Way ;
And Christ the Light, thy setting Sun,
Sinks ere thy morning is begun :
Haste, traveller, haste !

Awake, awake ! pursue thy way
With steady course while yet 'tis day ;
While thou art sleeping on the ground
Danger and darkness gather round :
Haste, traveller, haste !

The rising tempest sweeps the sky ;
The rains descend, the winds are high ;
The waters swell, and death and fear
Beset thy path, nor refuge near :
Haste, traveller, haste !

O yes! a shelter you may gain,
A covert from the wind and rain,
A hiding-place, a rest, a home,
A refuge from the wrath to come:
    Haste, traveller, haste!

Then linger not in all the plain;
Flee for thy life; the mountain gain;
Look not behind; make no delay;
O speed thee, speed thee on thy way:
    Haste, traveller, haste!

Poor, lost, benighted soul! art thou
Willing to find salvation now?
There yet is hope; hear mercy's call:
Truth! Life! Light! Way! in Christ is all!
    Haste to Him, haste!

      Collyer.

Forward.

Shall this life of mine be wasted?
 Shall this vineyard lie untill'd?
Shall true joy pass by untasted,
 And this soul remain unfill'd?

Shall the God-given hours be scatter'd
 Like the leaves upon the plain?
Shall the blossoms die unwater'd
 By the drops of heavenly rain?

Miscellaneous.

Shall I see each fair sun waking,
  And not feel it wakes for me—
Each glad morning brightly breaking,
  And not feel it breaks for me?

Shall I see the roses blowing,
  And not wish to bloom as they—
Holy fragrance round me throwing,
  Luring others on the way?

Shall I hear the free bird singing
  In the summer's stainless sky,
Far aloft its glad flight winging,
  And not seek to soar as high?

Shall this heart still spend its treasures
  On the things that fade and die?
Shall it court the hollow pleasures
  Of bewildering vanity?

Shall these lips of mine be idle?
  Shall I open them in vain?
Shall I not, with God's own bridle,
  Their frivolities restrain?

Shall these eyes of mine still wander?
  Or, no longer turn'd afar,
Fix a firmer gaze, and fonder,
  On the bright and morning Star?

Shall these feet of mine, delaying,
  Still in ways of sin be found,
Braving snares, and madly straying
  On the world's bewitching ground?

No; I was not born to trifle
    Life away in dreams or sin!
No; I must not, dare not stifle
    Longings such as these within!

Swiftly moving, upward, onward,
    Let my soul in faith be borne!
Calmly gazing, skyward, sunward,
    Let my eye unshrinking turn!

                                Horatius Bonar.

Arise and Depart.

BRETHREN, arise;
    Let us go hence!
        Defiled, polluted thus,
        This is no home for us;
        Till earth is purified,
        We may not here abide.
        We were not born for earth:
        The city of our birth,
        The better paradise,
        Is far above these skies.
        Upward then let us soar,
        Cleaving to dust no more!

Brethren, arise;
    Let us go hence!
        Death and the grave are here,
        The sick-bed and the bier.

The children of the tomb
May love this kindred gloom;
But we, the deathless band,
Must seek the deathless land.
The mortal here may rove:
The immortal dwell above.
Here we can only die:
Let us ascend on high.

Brethren, arise;
Let us go hence!
For we are weary here.
The ever-falling tear,
The ever-swelling sigh,
The sorrow ever nigh,
The sin still flowing on,
Creation's ceaseless groan,
The tumult near and far,
The universal war,
The sounds that never cease—
These are our weariness!

Brethren, arise;
Let us go hence!
This is not our abode;
Too far, too far from God!
The angels dwell not here:
There falls not on the ear
The everlasting song
From the celestial throng.

K

'Tis discord here alone ;
Earth's melody is gone :
Her harp lies broken now ;
Her praise has ceased to flow !

Brethren, arise ;
   Let us go hence !
      The New Jerusalem,
      Like a resplendent gem,
      Sends down its heavenly light,
      Attracting our dull sight.
      I see the bright ones wait
      At each fair pearly gate ;
      I hear their voices call ;
      I see the jasper wall,
      The clear, translucent gold,
      The glory all untold !

Brethren, arise ;
   Let us go hence !
      What are earth's joys and gems ?
      What are its diadems ?
      Our crowns are waiting us
      Within our Father's house.
      Our friends above the skies
      Are bidding us arise.
      Our Lord, He calls away
      To scenes of sweeter day
      Than this sad earth can know.
      Let us arise and go !

Horatius Bonar.

Jesus our Guide.

THE Saviour is our living Head:
  Where He appoints we go,
And will in Jesus' footsteps tread
  While dwelling here below.

His voice we know, and fain would hear,
  Directing us aright,
That we may never danger fear,
  But walk amid the light

Partakers of His heavenly grace,
  The same in mind and heart,
Not life nor death, nor time nor place,
  Shall make us ever part.

But closer to His side we'll cling,
  While life shall last—till death,
And wondrous loving-kindness sing
  With our expiring breath.

Henry Jennings.

God's Care.

THERE's not a bird, with lonely nest,
In pathless wood or mountain crest,
Nor meaner thing, which does not share,
O God, in Thy paternal care!

There's not a being now accurst
Who did not taste Thy goodness first;
And every joy the wicked see
Received its origin from Thee.

Each barren crag, each desert rude,
Holds Thee within its solitude;
And Thou dost bless the wanderer there,
Who makes his solitary prayer.

In busy mart and crowded street,
No less than in the still retreat,
Thou, Lord, art near, our souls to bless
With all a parent's tenderness!

And every moment still doth bring
Thy blessings on its loaded wing;
Widely they spread through earth and sky,
And last to all eternity!

Through all creation let Thy name
Be echoed with a glad acclaim!
That let the grateful churches sing;
With that let heaven for ever ring!

And we, where'er our lot is cast,
While life and thought and feeling last,
Through all our years, in every place,
Will bless Thee for Thy boundless grace!

Hon. Baptist Wriothesley Noel.

Principalities and Powers subject to Christ.

Now far above the starry skies,
Our Jesus fills His brighter throne,
Invisible to mortal eyes,
But not to humble faith unknown.

The countless hosts that round Him stand,
The subjects of His sov'reign power,
Fly through the world at His command,
Or prostrate at His feet adore.

Satan and all his rebel crew
That raged to pull His kingdom down,
Crush'd by His hand, in ruin now
Lie trembling at His awful frown.

His name above all creatures great,
He all sustains and all controls!
Yet from His high, exalted state
Looks kindly down on humble souls.

Though in the glories He possess'd,
Long ere this world or time began,
He shines the Son of God confess'd,
Yet owns Himself the Son of man.

Here once in agonies He died :
Now in the heavens He ever lives ;
Of joy there pours the eternal tide,
Here saves the sinner who believes.

All hail ! Thou great Immanuel, hail !
Ten thousand blessings on Thy name !
While thus Thy wondrous love we tell,
Our bosoms feel the sacred flame.

Come, quickly come, immortal King !
On earth Thy regal honours raise;
The full salvation, promised, bring ;
Then every tongue shall sing Thy praise !
Turner.

Supplicating.

Jesus, full of all compassion,
    Hear Thy humble suppliant's cry ;
Let me know Thy great salvation :
    See ! I languish, faint, and die.

Guilty, but with heart relenting,
    Overwhelm'd with helpless grief,
Prostrate at Thy feet repenting,
    Send, O send me quick relief!

Whither should a wretch be flying,
    But to Him who comfort gives ?
Whither, from the dread of dying,
    But to Him who ever lives ?

While I view Thee, wounded, grieving,
    Breathless on the cursèd tree,
Fain I'd feel my heart believing
    That Thou sufferedst thus for me.

With Thy righteousness and Spirit,
    I am more than angels blest ;
Heir with Thee, all things inherit—
    Peace, and joy, and endless rest.

Without Thee, the world possessing,
    I should be a wretch undone,
Search through heaven, the land of blessing,
    Seeking good and finding none.

Hear, then, blessed Saviour, hear me :
  My soul cleaveth to the dust.
Send the Comforter to cheer me :
  Lo ! in Thee I put my trust.

On the word Thy blood hath sealèd
  Hangs my everlasting all :
Let Thy arm be now revealèd ;
  Stay, O stay me, lest I fall !

In the world of endless ruin
  Let it never, Lord, be said,
" Here's a soul that perish'd, suing
  For the boasted Saviour's aid !"

Saved : the deed shall spread new glory
  Through the shining realms above !
Angels sing the pleasing story,
  All enraptured with Thy love !

                 Turner.

Longing for an Interest in Christ.

  Gracious Lord ! incline Thine ear !
  My requests vouchsafe to hear.
  Hear my never-ceasing cry :
  Give me Christ, or else I die.

  Wealth and honour I disdain ;
  Earthly comforts, Lord, are vain :
  These can never satisfy.
  Give me Christ, or else I die.

Lord, deny me what Thou wilt,
Only ease me of my guilt.
Suppliant at Thy feet I lie :
Give me Christ, or else I die.

All unholy and unclean,
I am nothing else but sin.
On Thy mercy I rely :
Give me Christ, or else I die.

Thou dost freely save the lost!
In Thy grace alone I trust.
With my earnest suit comply :
Give me Christ, or else I die.

Thou dost promise to forgive
All who in Thy Son believe.
Lord, I know Thou canst not lie :
Give me Christ, or else I die.

Father, does Thy justice frown?
Let me shelter in Thy Son!
Jesus, to Thy arms I fly :
Come and save me, or I die.

Anon.

Things Hoped for.

THESE are the crowns that we shall wear
   When all thy saints are crown'd :
These are the palms that we shall bear
   On yonder holy ground.

Far off as yet, reserved in heaven,
   Above that veiling sky,
They sparkle, like the star of even,
   To hope's far-piercing eye.

These are the robes, unsoil'd and white,
   Which then we shall put on,
When, foremost 'mong the sons of light,
   We sit on yonder throne.

That city with the jewell'd crest,
   Like some new-lighted sun ;
A blaze of burning amethyst,
   Ten thousand orbs in one—

That is the city of the saints,
   Where we so soon shall stand,
When we shall strike these desert-tents,
   And quit this desert-sand.

These are the everlasting hills,
   With summits bathed in day,
The slopes down which the living rills,
   Soft-lapsing, take their way.

Fair vision ! how thy distant gleam
   Brightens time's saddest hue !
Far fairer than the fairest dream,
   And yet so strangely true !

Fair vision! how thou liftest up
  The drooping brow and eye;
With the calm joy of thy sure hope
  Fixing our souls on high!

Thy light makes even the darkest page
  In memory's scroll grow fair;
Blanching the lines which tears and age
  Had only deepen'd there.

With thee in view, the rugged slope
  Becomes a level way,
Smoothed by the magic of thy hope,
  And gladden'd by thy ray.

With thee in view, how poor appear
  The world's most winning smiles!
Vain is the tempter's subtlest snare,
  And vain hell's varied wiles.

Time's glory fades; its beauty now
  Has ceased to lure or blind:
Each gay enchantment here below
  Has lost its power to bind.
                        Horatius Bonar.

The Successful Resolve.

Come, humble sinner, in whose breast
  A thousand thoughts revolve,
Come, with your guilt and fear opprest,
  And make this last resolve :—

"I'll go to Jesus, though my sin
    Hath like a mountain rose:
I know His courts; I'll enter in,
    Whatever may oppose.

"Prostrate I'll lie before His throne,
    And there my guilt confess:
I'll tell Him I'm a wretch undone,
    Without His sov'reign grace.

"I'll to the gracious King approach,
    Whose sceptre pardon gives:
Perhaps He may command my touch,
    And then the suppliant lives.

"Perhaps He will admit my plea,
    Perhaps will hear my prayer;
But if I perish, I will pray,
    And perish only there.

"I can but perish if I go:
    I am resolved to try;
For if I stay away, I know
    I must for ever die.

"But if I die with mercy sought,
    When I the King have tried,
This were to die (delightful thought!)
    As sinner never died."

                              Anon.

Gwell pwyll mac awr.

I HEAR the counsel of a Friend,
And to His soothing voice attend :
Come, sinners, come, though blind and poor;
Come, buy from My unbounded store.

Come as you are, and try Me now;
Approach My throne, and humbly bow ;
Come and receive, and I will give
A contrite mind, that you may live.

Though wretched, come for that bright dress,
My perfect, spotless righteousness ;
That glorious robe, so richly dyed
In My own blood, your shame to hide.

Lay all your filthy rags aside,
And I will clothe you as My bride ;
I will bestow your wedding dress,
The robe of perfect righteousness.

Henry Jennings.

Holy Importunity.

Lord, I cannot let Thee go
Till a blessing Thou bestow.
Do not turn away Thy face:
Mine's an urgent, pressing case.

Dost Thou ask me who I am?
Ah, my Lord, Thou know'st my name!
Yet the question gives a plea
To support my suit with Thee.

Thou didst once a wretch behold,
In rebellion blindly bold,
Scorn Thy grace, Thy power defy:
That poor rebel, Lord, was I.

Once a sinner near despair
Sought Thy mercy-seat by prayer;
Mercy heard and set him free:
Lord, that mercy came to me.

Many days have pass'd since then,
Many changes I have seen,
Yet have been upheld till now:
Who could hold me up but Thou?

Thou hast help'd in every need:
This emboldens me to plead,
After so much mercy past,
Canst Thou let me sink at last?

No; I must maintain my hold:
'Tis Thy goodness makes me bold.
I can no denial take,
When I plead for Jesus' sake.

Anon.

Tempted, but Flying to Christ.

Jesus, lover of my soul,
  Let me to Thy bosom fly,
While the raging billows roll,
  While the tempest still is high !
Hide me, O my Saviour, hide,
  Till the storm of life is past;
Safe into the haven guide :
  O receive my soul at last !

Other refuge have I none :
  Hangs my helpless soul on Thee !
Leave, ah ! leave me not alone :
  Still support and comfort me !
All my trust on Thee is stay'd ;
  All my help from Thee I bring :
Cover my defenceless head
  With the shadow of Thy wing.

Thou, O Christ, art all I want ;
  All in all in Thee I find :
Raise the fallen, cheer the faint,
  Heal the sick, and lead the blind.
Just and holy is Thy name :
  I am all unrighteousness.
Vile and full of sin I am :
  Thou art full of truth and grace.

Plenteous grace with Thee is found—
   Grace to pardon all my sin :
Let the healing streams abound ;
   Make and keep me pure within.
Thou of life the Fountain art :
   Freely let me take of Thee !
Spring Thou up within my heart ;
   Rise to all eternity !

Wesley.

Sacramental 𝔥𝔶𝔪𝔫.

Jesus, O word divinely sweet !
   How charming is the sound !
What joyful news, what heavenly sense,
   In that dear name is found !

Our souls, all guilty and condemn'd,
   In hopeless fetters lay ;
Our souls, with numerous sins depraved,
   To death and hell a prey.

Jesus, to purge away this guilt,
   A willing victim fell,
And on His cross triumphant broke
   The bands of death and hell.

Our foes were mighty to destroy :
   He mighty was to save.
He died, but could not long be held
   A prisoner in the grave.

Jesus, who mighty art to save,
    Still push Thy conquests on :
Extend the triumphs of Thy cross
    Where'er the sun has shone.

O Captain of salvation, make
    Thy power and mercy known,
Till crowds of willing converts come
    And worship at Thy throne.

                       Stennett.

Social Worship.

How charming is the place
    Where my Redeemer, God,
Unveils the beauties of His face,
    And sheds His love abroad !

Not the fair palaces
    To which the great resort
Are once to be compared with this,
    Where Jesus holds His court.

Here, on the mercy-seat,
    With radiant glory crown'd,
Our joyful eyes behold Him sit,
    And smile on all around.

To Him their prayers and cries
    Each humble soul presents :
He listens to their broken sighs,
    And grants them all their wants

To them His sovereign will
He graciously imparts;
And in return accepts, with smiles,
The tribute of their hearts.

Give me, O Lord, a place
Within Thy blest abode,
Among the children of Thy grace,
The servants of my God.

Stennett.

The Friend.

THERE is a star in yonder sky,
Above all stars it seems to shine,
'Tis long since first it fix'd my eye,
And I have learn'd to call it mine.

It rose out of my own blue sea,
Then pass'd above those mountains green,
Moving along all placidly,
As if it loved to watch the scene.

Far up the heavens it floated slow,
Gleaming across yon solemn tower,
As if it loved the scene below;
A willing lingerer hour by hour.

It seemed to take its place each night,
A sentinel to guard my rest,
An eye of love and gentle light,
Pouring sweet thoughts into my breast.

In through my lattice, as I lay
Half-soothed to sleep, it nightly shone;
And, as I gazed upon its ray,
I felt that I was not alone.

What tears that gentle star has dried;
What joy that sparkling orb has given;
Thoughts for this earth too high, too wide,
Dreams of its own all-radiant heaven.

It spoke of day beyond this night,
In the glad land where all is fair;
It pointed to the home of light,
And bid me rest my spirit there.

It spoke of Him whose love is light,
Whose death is life, whose cross is peace,
Whose favour is the star of night,
The source and pledge of endless bliss.

May I not love that star on high?
May not its light the fairest seem?
May I not trace a loving eye,
A kindly smile, in every beam?

Horatius Bonar.

The Great Question Answered.

Is there, in heaven or earth, who can
    A wretched mortal save?
Make a poor leprous sinner clean?
    Redeem a helpless slave?

Who can appease an angry God?
  Relieve a burden'd mind?
In whom a soul, o'erwhelm'd with guilt,
  May ease and safety find?

Yes, there is One, who dwells on high,
  That can do this and more;
A Being of unbounded love
  And uncontrollèd power.

Immanuel is His name; who once,
  Upon the accursèd tree,
Bore the vast weight of all their sins
  Who, burden'd, to Him flee.

But now He lives, He ever lives,
  And pleads what He hath done;
While God ten thousand crimes forgives,
  Through His atoning Son.

Jesus, I to Thy feet repair,
  And there will prostrate lie:
Be Thou propitious to my prayer,
  And I shall never die.
                              Beddome, altered.

Lines on a Sweet Babe.

Sweet babe, how very innocent art thou!
How smooth and beautiful thy sun-lit brow!
How gentle is thy sleep! why, scarce a sigh!
Thou precious little treasure from on high!

In thee I see the great Creator's pow'r,
Who cares for, watches, guards thee, hour by hour :
In infant form I see the skill Divine,
Which will still brighter, brighter, brighter shine.

How priceless a boon from heaven thou art,
From which no loving friend would ever part !
I love thee, but some love thee more than I :
They'd live for thee, and for thee they would die.

I love to tend and show thee every care,
To waft to heaven a grateful prayer,
That life preservèd, and life now given,
May be to Jesus Christ for ever riven.

I love to see thy pretty babe-like smile,
As I caress and fondle thee awhile ;
I love to fold thee gently to my breast,
And hush thee, sweetest babe, to sweetest rest.

I know that angels watch thee day by day ;
I know that they will guide, and with thee stay ;
I once more kiss thy little hand and face,
And supplicate for thee the Father's grace.

Farewell, dear child : may you all blessings share,
In life, in death, beyond this world of care.
Farewell, until we meet at His right hand,
Where countless myriads will for ever stand.

Henry Jennings.

The Lord's Prayer.

Our Father, whose eternal sway
The bright angelic hosts obey,
   O lend a pitying ear!
When on Thy awful name we call,
And at Thy feet submissive fall,
   O condescend to hear!

Far may Thy glorious reign extend:
May rebels to Thy sceptre bend,
   And yield to sovereign love.
May we take pleasure to fulfil
The sacred dictates of Thy will,
   As angels do above.

From Thy kind hand each temporal good,
Our raiment and our daily food,
   In rich abundance come.
Lord, give us still a fresh supply:
If Thou withhold Thy hand, we die,
   And fill the silent tomb.

Pardon our sins, O God, that rise,
And call for vengeance from the skies;
   And, while we are forgiven,
Grant that revenge may never rest,
Nor malice harbour in that breast
   That feels the love of heaven.

Protect us in the dangerous hour,
And from the wily tempter's power
　O set our spirits free!
And, if temptation should assail,
May mighty grace o'er all prevail,
　And lead our hearts to Thee.

Thine is the power; to Thee belongs
The constant tribute of our songs:
　All glory to Thy name.
Let every creature join our lays,
In one resounding act of praise
　Thy wonders to proclaim.

J. Straphan.

Pray for Us.

MARK'D as the purpose of the skies,
This promise meets our anxious eyes:
That heathen lands the Lord shall know,
And, warm with faith, each bosom glow.

Even now the hallow'd scenes appear:
Even now unfolds the promised year:
Lo! distant shores Thy heralds trace,
And bear the tidings of Thy grace.

'Mid burning climes and frozen plains,
Where pagan darkness brooding reigns,
Lord! mark their steps, their fears subdue,
And nerve their arm, and clear their view.

When, worn by toil, their spirits fail,
Bid them the glorious future hail;
Bid them the crown of life survey,
And onward urge their conquering way.

Hon. Baptist Wriothesley Noel.

God's Love and Mercy.

Ere God had built the mountains,
    Or raised the fruitful hills,
Before He fill'd the fountains
    That feed the running rills,
In Me, from everlasting,
    The wonderful I AM
Found pleasures never wasting;
    And Wisdom is My name.

When, like a tent to dwell in,
    He spread the skies abroad,
And swathed about the swelling
    Of ocean's mighty flood,
He wrought by weight and measure
    And I was with Him then;
Myself the Father's pleasure,
    And Mine the sons of men.

Thus Wisdom's words discover
    Thy glory and Thy grace,
Thou everlasting lover
    Of our unworthy race!

Thy gracious eye survey'd us
   Ere stars were seen above;
In wisdom Thou hast made us,
   And died for us in love.

And couldst Thou be delighted
   With creatures such as we,
Who, when we saw Thee, slighted,
   And nail'd Thee to a tree?
Unfathomable wonder,
   And mystery Divine!
The voice that speaks in thunder
   Says, "Sinner, I am thine!"

Anon.

False and True Pleasure.

How vain a thought is bliss below!
   'Tis all an airy dream:
How empty are the joys that flow
   On pleasure's smiling stream!

Transparent now, and all serene,
   The gentle current flows:
While fancy draws the flatt'ring scene
   How fair the landscape shows!

But soon its transient charms decay,
   When ruffling tempests blow;
The soft delusions fleet away,
   And pleasure ends in woe.

O let my nobler wishes soar
    Beyond these seats of night,
In heav'n substantial bliss explore,
    And permanent delight.

There pleasure flows for ever clear!
    And, rising to the view,
Such dazzling scenes of joy appear
    As fancy never drew.

No fleeting landscape cheats the gaze,
    Nor airy form beguiles,
But everlasting bliss displays
    Her undissembled smiles.

                          Steele.

The Christian's Happy State.

How happy is the Christian's state!
    His sins are all forgiv'n;
A cheering ray confirms the grace,
    And lifts his hopes to heav'n.

Though in the rugged path of life
    He heaves the pensive sigh,
Yet, trusting in his God, he finds
    Deliv'ring grace is nigh.

If, to prevent his wand'ring steps,
    He feels the chast'ning rod,
The gentle stroke shall bring him back
    To his forgiving God.

And when the welcome message comes,
    To call his soul away,
His soul in raptures shall ascend
    To everlasting day.
                          B. M. Bristol Col.

Links.

ARE there not voices strangely sweet,
And tones of music strangely dear?
So lovingly the soul they greet;
So kindly steal they on the ear.

We know not why they strike so deep:
We cannot tell the secret spring
Within us which they wake from sleep,
Nor how such thoughts their notes can bring.

We ask not why or how they thrill
So keenly through the inmost soul;
Nor why, when ceased, we listen still,
As though they yet upon us stole.

We feel the sweetness of the voice;
We love the richness of the tone:
It makes us sorrow or rejoice,
Compelling us its power to own.

Are there not words, too, strangely sweet,
Thoughts, musings, memories strangely dear?
So lovingly the soul they greet!
So gently steal they on the ear!

Common the words may be, and weak;
The passing stranger owns them not;
To other ears in vain they speak,
Unknown, unrelished, or forgot.

Rich in old thoughts, these words appear
Part of our being's mighty whole;
Link'd with our life's strange story here,
Knit to each feeling of our soul.

Link'd with the scenes of days gone past,
With all life's earnest hopes and fears;
Link'd with the smiles that did not last,
The joys and griefs of faded years.

Link'd with old dreams once dreamt in youth,
When dreams were gladder, truer things,
When each night's vision of bright truth
Lent to each buoyant day its wings.

Link'd with the whisper of the trees,
When summer-eves were fair and still;
Set to the music of the breeze,
Or murmur of the twilight rill.

Link'd with some scene of sacred calm,
Of holy places, holy days;
Link'd with the prayer, the hymn, the psalm,
The multitude's glad voice of praise.

Link'd with the names of holy men,
Martyr, or saint, or brother dear;
Some parted, ne'er to meet again,
Some still our fellow-pilgrims here.

Link'd with that Name of names, the name
Of Him who bought us with His blood,
Who bore for us the wrath and shame,
The Virgin's Son, the Christ of God.

Horatius Bonar.

Peace to the Returning Penitent.

Sweet is the friendly voice which speaks
    The words of life and peace ;
Which bids the penitent rejoice,
    And sin and sorrow cease.

No healing balm on earth like this
    Can cheer the contrite heart,
No flatt'ring dreams of earthly bliss
    Such pure delight impart.

Thou still art merciful and kind ;
    Thy mercy, Lord, reveal :
The broken heart 'tis Thou canst bind,
    The wounded spirit heal.

Let Thy bright presence, Lord, restore
    Peace to my anxious breast :
Conduct me to the path that leads
    To everlasting rest.

Jervis.

Heavenward.

FAR from these narrow scenes of night
    Unbounded glories rise,
And realms of infinite delight,
    Unknown to mortal eyes.

Fair distant land! could mortal eyes
    But half its joys explore,
How would our spirits long to rise,
    And dwell on earth no more!

There pain and sickness never come,
    And grief no more complains;
Health triumphs in immortal bloom,
    And endless pleasure reigns.

No cloud those blissful regions know,
    For ever bright and fair;
For sin, the source of mortal woe,
    Can never enter there.

There no alternate night is known,
    Nor sun's faint, sickly ray;
But glory from the sacred throne
    Spreads everlasting day.

The glorious Monarch there displays
    His beams of wondrous grace;
His happy subjects sing His praise,
    And bow before His face.

O may the heavenly prospect fire
    Our hearts with ardent love,
Till wings of faith and strong desire
    Bear every thought above!

Prepare us, Lord, by grace Divine,
    For Thy bright courts on high;
Then bid our spirits rise, and join
    The chorus of the sky.

Steele.

The Cross.

BENEATH Thy cross I lay me down,
And mourn to see Thy bloody crown.
Love drops in blood from every vein:
Love is the spring of all His pain.

Here, Jesus, I shall ever stay,
And spend my longing hours away,
Think on Thy bleeding wounds and pain,
And contemplate Thy woes again.

The rage of Satan and of sin,
Of foes without and fears within,
Shall ne'er my conquering soul remove,
Or from Thy cross, or from Thy love.

Secured from harms beneath Thy shade,
Here death and hell shall ne'er invade:
Nor Sinai, with its thundering noise,
Shall e'er disturb my happier joys.

O unmolested, happy rest !
Where inward fears are all supprest :
Here I shall love, and live secure,
And patiently my cross endure.

William Williams.

Resurrection.

WE sing His love who once was slain,
Who soon o'er death revived again,
That all His saints through Him might have
Eternal conquests o'er the grave.
　　Soon shall the trumpet sound, and we
　　Shall rise to immortality.

The saints who now with Jesus sleep
His own almighty power shall keep,
Till dawns the bright, illustrious day
When death itself shall die away :
　　Soon shall the trumpet sound, and we
　　Shall rise to immortality.

How loud shall our glad voices sing
When Christ His risen saints shall bring,
From beds of dust and silent clay,
To realms of everlasting day !
　　Soon shall the trumpet sound, and we
　　Shall rise to immortality.

When Jesus we in glory meet
Our utmost joys shall be complete;
When landed on that heavenly shore
Death and the curse will be no more :
   Soon shall the trumpet sound, and we
   Shall rise to immortality.

Hasten, dear Lord, the glorious day,
And this delightful scene display,
When all Thy saints from death shall rise,
Raptured in bliss, beyond the skies!
   Soon shall the trumpet sound, and we
   Shall rise to immortality.

Rowland Hill.

𝔥𝔢𝔞𝔳𝔢𝔫.

O HAPPY saints, who dwell in light,
And walk with Jesus clothed in white !
Safe landed on that peaceful shore
Where pilgrims meet to part no more.

Released from sin, and toil, and grief,
Death was their gate to endless life ;
An open cage to let them fly,
And build their happy nest on high.

And now they range the heav'nly plains,
And sing their hymns in melting strains ;
And now their souls begin to prove
The heights and depths of Jesus' love.

They gaze upon His beauteous face,
His lovely mind and charming grace,
And, gazing hard with ravish'd eyes,
His form they catch, and taste His joys.

He cheers them with eternal smile :
They sing hosannahs all the while ;
Or, overwhelm'd with rapture sweet,
Sink down adoring at His feet.

Ah! Lord, with tardy steps I creep,
And sometimes sing, and sometimes weep ;
Yet strip me of this house of clay,
And I will sing as loud as they.

Berridge.

𝕿𝖍𝖊 𝕱𝖊𝖙𝖙𝖊𝖗𝖊𝖉 𝕸𝖎𝖓𝖉.

Ah! why should this immortal mind,
Enslaved by sense, be thus confined,
　　And never, never rise?
Why, thus amused with empty toys,
And soothed with visionary joys,
　　Forget her native skies?

The mind was form'd to mount sublime,
Beyond the narrow bounds of time,
　　To everlasting things ;
But earthly vapours cloud her sight,
And hang, with cold, oppressive weight,
　　Upon her drooping wings.

M

The world employs its various snares,
Of hopes and pleasures, pains and cares,
   And chain'd to earth I lie:
When shall my fetter'd pow'rs be free,
And leave these seats of vanity,
   And upward learn to fly?

Bright scenes of bliss, unclouded skies,
Invite my soul: O! could I rise,
   Nor leave a thought below,
I'd bid farewell to anxious care,
And say to ev'ry tempting snare,
   Heav'n calls, and I must go.

Heav'n calls! and can I yet delay?
Can aught on earth engage my stay?
   Ah! wretched, ling'ring heart!
Come, Lord, with strength, and life, and light,
Assist and guide my upward flight,
   And bid the world depart.

Steele.

The Sabbath Day.

Hail, Sabbath morning, brightest, best,
Above all days emblem of rest!
Day when all men from labour cease:
O happy day of inward peace!

How gladly do we hail this day—
Ev'n the first and earliest ray
Of morning light, which drives away
Night's shades, and turns them into day.

How happy do we feel when all
Before the family altar fall ;
And parents, children, all can say,
How sacred is this hour and day !

How quickly do we wend our way,
Where the saints meet to praise and pray ;
Where songs of praise still higher rise,
Beyond all worlds, beyond the skies.

How joyful are our feelings there,
When banish'd are our fears and care,
And, borne on wings of faith, we rise,
To seize th' eternal crown, the prize.

Henry Jennings.

𝔗𝔥𝔢 𝔏𝔞𝔫𝔡 𝔬𝔣 𝔏𝔦𝔤𝔥𝔱.

That clime is not like this dull clime of ours :
  All, all is brightness there ;
A sweeter influence breathes around its flowers,
  And a far milder air.
No calm below is like that calm above ;
No region here is like that realm of love :
Earth's softest spring ne'er shed so soft a light ;
Earth's brightest summer never shone so bright.

That sky is not like this sad sky of ours,
     Tinged with earth's change and care :
No shadow dims it, and no rain-cloud lowers ;
     No broken sunshine there !
One everlasting stretch of azure pours
Its stainless splendour o'er these sinless shores :
For there Jehovah shines with heavenly ray,
There Jesus reigns, dispensing endless day.

Those dwellers there are not like these of earth—
     No mortal stain they bear—
And yet they seem of kindred blood and birth :
     Whence, and how came they there ?
Earth was their native soil : from sin and shame,
Through tribulation, they to glory came ;
Bond-slaves deliver'd from sin's crushing load,
Brands pluck'd from burning by the hand of God.

Those robes of theirs are not like these below :
     No angel's half so bright !
Whence came that beauty, whence that living glow ?
     Whence came that radiant white ?
Wash'd in the blood of the atoning Lamb,
Fair as the light those robes of theirs became,
And now, all tears wiped off from every eye,
They wander where the freshest pastures lie,
Through all the nightless day of that unfading sky !

Horatius Bonar.

Day=spring.

THE loving morn is springing
　From night's unloving gloom;
And earth seems now arising
　In beauty from the tomb.

See daylight far above us,
　Tinging each cloudy wreath,
Ere it showers itself in splendour
　Upon the plain beneath.

'Tis sparkling on the mountain-peak;
　'Tis hurrying down the vale;
'Tis bursting through the forest-boughs;
　'Tis fresh'ning in the gale.

'Tis mingling with the river's smile;
　'Tis glist'ning in the dew;
'Tis flinging far its silver net,
　O'er ocean's braided blue.

'Tis blushing o'er the meadow's gold;
　'Tis alighting on the flower,
Unfolding every gentle bud
　To the gladness of the hour.

'Tis gilding the old ruin's moss;
　'Tis gleaming from the spire;
And through the crumbling window-shafts
　It shoots its living fire.

'Tis quivering in the village smoke
　　That curls the low roof o'er;
It beats against the castle gate,
　　And at the cottage door.

O'er the churchyard it is resting,
　　On stone, and grass, and mould;
Giving voice to each gray tombstone,
　　As to Memnon's harp of old.

O the gay burst of beauty
　　That is flushing over earth,
And calling forth its millions
　　To holy morning mirth!

Yet look we for a sunrise
　　More beautiful than this;
And watch we for a dawning
　　Of purer light and bliss;

When a far fairer morning
　　O'er greener hills shall rise,
And a far fresher sunlight
　　Look down from bluer skies.

Is not creation weary?
　　Has sin not reign'd too long?
Hear, Lord, Thy church's pleading:
　　Come, end her day of wrong!

Horatius Bonar.

On the Death of a Friend.

While to the grave our friends are borne,
    Around their cold remains
How all the tender passions mourn,
    And each fond heart complains!

But down to earth, alas! in vain
    We bend our weeping eyes.
Ah! let us leave these seats of pain,
    And upward learn to rise.

Hope cheerful smiles amid the gloom,
    And beams a healing ray,
And guides us from the darksome tomb
    To realms of endless day.

Jesus, who left His blest abode
    (Amazing grace!) to die,
Mark'd, when he rose, the shining road
    To His bright courts on high.

To those bright courts when hope ascends
    The tears forget to flow:
Hope views our absent, happy friends,
    And calms the swelling woe.

Then let our hearts repine no more
    That earthly comfort dies;
But lasting happiness explore,
    And ask it from the skies.

Steele.

Not very Far.

Surely, yon heaven, where angels see God's face,
   Is not so distant as we deem
From this low earth.   'Tis but a little space,
   The narrow crossing of a slender stream ;
'Tis but a veil, which winds might blow aside :
Yes, these are all that us of earth divide
From the bright dwelling of the glorified,
   The land of which I dream !

These peaks are nearer heaven than earth below :
   These hills are higher than they seem.
'Tis not the clouds they touch, nor the soft brow
   Of the o'er-bending azure, as we deem :
'Tis the blue floor of heaven that they up-bear ;
And, like some old and wildly rugged stair,
They lift us to the land where all is fair,
   The land of which I dream !

These ocean waves, in their unmeasured sweep,
   Are brighter, bluer than they seem ;
True image here of the celestial deep,
   Fed from the fulness of the unfailing stream ;
Heaven's glassy sea of everlasting rest,
With not a breath to stir its silent breast ;
The sea that laves the land where all are blest,
   The land of which I dream !

And these keen stars, the bridal gems of night,
  Are purer, lovelier than they seem ;
Fill'd from the inner fountain of deep light,
  They pour down heaven's own beam ;
Clear speaking from their throne of glorious blue,
In accents ever ancient, ever new,
Of the glad home above, beyond our view,
  The land of which I dream !

This life of ours, these lingering years of earth,
  Are briefer, swifter than they seem :
A little while, and the great second birth
  Of time shall come, the prophet's ancient theme !
Then He, the King, the Judge, at length shall come,
And for this desert, where we sadly roam,
Shall give the kingdom for our endless home,
  The land of which I dream !

Horatius Bonar.

Bridegroom and Husband.

JESUS, the heavenly Lover, gave
His life my wretched soul to save :
Resolved to make His mercy known,
He kindly claims me for His own.

Rebellious, I against Him strove,
Till melted and constrain'd by love.
With sin and self I freely part :
The heavenly Bridegroom wins my heart.

My guilt, my wretchedness, He knows,
Yet takes and owns me for His spouse;
My debts He pays, and sets me free,
And makes His riches o'er to me.

My filthy rags are laid aside:
He clothes me as becomes His bride;
Himself bestows my wedding-dress,
The robe of perfect righteousness.

Lost in astonishment, I see,
Jesus, Thy boundless love to me:
With angels I Thy grace adore,
And long to love and praise Thee more.

Since Thou wilt take me for Thy bride,
O Saviour, keep me near Thy side!
I fain would give Thee all my heart,
Nor ever from my Lord depart.

Fawcett.

Intercession of Christ.

Awake, sweet gratitude, and sing
　Th' ascended Saviour's love:
Sing how He lives to carry on
　His people's cause above.

With cries and tears He offer'd up
　His humble suit below;
But with authority He asks,
　Enthroned in glory, now.

For all that come to God by Him
    Salvation He demands ;
Points to their names upon His breast,
    And spreads His wounded hands.

His sweet atoning sacrifice
    Gives sanction to His claim :
" Father, I will that all My saints
    Be with Me where I am :

" By their salvation recompense
    The sorrows I endured ;
Just to the merits of Thy Son,
    And faithful to Thy word."

Eternal life, at His request,
    To every saint is given;
Safety below, and, after death,
    The plenitude of heaven.

Founded on right, Thy prayer avails ;
    The Father smiles on Thee ;
And now Thou in Thy kingdom art,
    Dear Lord, remember me.

Let the much incense of Thy prayer
    In my behalf ascend ;
And, as its virtue, so my praise
    Shall never, never end.

                Toplady.

Jesus Seen of Angels.

Beyond the glitt'ring starry skies,
  Far as th' eternal hills,
There, in the boundless worlds of light,
  Our dear Redeemer dwells.

Immortal angels, bright and fair,
  In countless armies shine!
At His right hand, with golden harps,
  They offer songs Divine.

" Hail, Prince !" they cry, " for ever hail,
  Whose unexampled love
Moved Thee to quit those glorious realms
  And royalties above."

And whilst He stoop'd on earth to dwell
  And suffer'd rude disdain,
They cast their honours at His feet,
  And waited in His train.

In all His toils and dangerous paths
  They did His steps attend,
Oft paused, and wonder'd how at last
  This scene of love would end.

And when the powers of hell combined
  To fill His cup of woe,
Their pitying eyes beheld His tears
  In bloody anguish flow.

As on the tott'ring tree He hung,
　　And darkness veil'd the sky,
They saw, aghast, that awful sight,
　　The LORD OF GLORY DIE!

Anon He bursts the gates of death,
　　Subdues the tyrant's power:
They saw th' illustrious Conqueror rise,
　　And hail'd the blessed hour.

They brought His chariot from above,
　　To bear Him to His throne;
Clapp'd their triumphant wings, and cried,
　　" THE GLORIOUS WORK IS DONE."

My soul the joyful triumph feels,
　　And thinks the moments long
Ere she her Saviour's glory sees,
　　And joins the rapturous song.

Anon.

Christ the Pearl of Great Price.

YE glitt'ring toys of earth, adieu:
　　A nobler choice be mine.
A real prize attracts my view,
　　A treasure all Divine.

Begone, unworthy of my cares,
　　Ye specious baits of sense:
Inestimable worth appears
　　The pearl of price immense.

Heavenly Melodies.

Jesus, to multitudes unknown,
  O name Divinely sweet!
Jesus, in Thee, in Thee alone,
  Wealth, honour, pleasure meet.

Should both the Indies, at my call,
  Their boasted stores resign,
With joy I would renounce them all,
  For leave to call Thee mine.

Should earth's vain treasures all depart,
  Of this dear gift possest,
I'd clasp it to my joyful heart,
  And be for ever blest.

Dear Sov'reign of my soul's desires,
  Thy love is bliss Divine:
Accept the wish that love inspires,
  And bid me call Thee mine.

Steele.

Inconstancy in Religion.

Perpetual source of light and grace,
  We hail Thy sacred name:
Through ev'ry year's revolving round
  Thy goodness is the same.

On us, all worthless as we are,
  Its wondrous mercy pours;
Sure as the heav'ns' establish'd course,
  And plenteous as the show'rs.

Inconstant service we repay,
  And treach'rous vows renew;
False as the morning's scatt'ring cloud,
  And transient as the dew.

In flowing tears our guilt we mourn,
  And loud implore Thy grace,
To bear our feeble footsteps on
  In all Thy righteous ways.

Arm'd with this energy Divine,
  Our souls shall steadfast move,
And with increasing transport press
  On to Thy courts above.

So by Thy pow'r the morning sun
  Pursues his radiant way,
Brightens each moment in his race,
  And shines to perfect day.

Doddridge.

The Struggle between Faith and Unbelief.

HEAL us, Emmanuel: here we are
  Waiting to feel Thy touch;
Deep wounded souls to Thee repair,
  And, Saviour, we are such.

Our faith is feeble, we confess;
  We faintly trust Thy word;
But wilt Thou pity us the less?
  Be that far from Thee, Lord!

Remember him who once applied
   With trembling for relief.
"Lord, I believe," with tears, he cried:
   "O help my unbelief."

She, too, who touch'd Thee in the press,
   And healing virtue stole,
Was answer'd, "Daughter, go in peace:
   Thy faith hath made thee whole."

Conceal'd amid the gath'ring throng,
   She would have shunn'd Thy view,
And if her faith was firm and strong,
   Had strong misgivings too.

Like her, with hopes and fears we come
   To touch Thee if we may:
O send us not despairing home;
   Send none unheal'd away.

Cowper.

God our Portion.

When Israel, by Divine command,
   The pathless desert trod,
They found, though 'twas a barren land,
   A sure resource in God.

A cloudy pillar mark'd their road,
   And screen'd them from the heat;
From the hard rocks their water flow'd,
   And manna was their meat.

Like them, we have a rest in view,
  Secure from adverse powers :
Like them, we pass a desert too ;
  And Israel's God is ours.

His word a light before us spreads
  By which our path we see :
His love, a banner o'er our heads,
  From harm preserves us free.

Jesus, the Bread of Life, is given
  To be our daily food :
We drink a wondrous stream from heaven ;
  'Tis water, wine, and blood.

Lord ! 'tis enough ! I ask no more :
  These blessings are Divine.
I envy not the worldling's store
  If Christ and heaven are mine.

                              Newton.

Living by Faith in Christ, etc.

My Jesus, while in mortal flesh
  I hold my frail abode,
Still would my spirit rest on Thee,
  Its Saviour and its God.

By hourly faith in Thee I live,
  Midst all my griefs and snares ;
And death, encounter'd in Thy sight,
  No form of horror wears.

                              N

Heavenly Melodies.

Yes, Thou hast loved this sinful worm,
    Hast giv'n Thyself for me;
Hast brought me from eternal death,
    Nail'd to the bloody tre.

On Thy dear cross I fix my eyes;
    Then raise them to Thy seat,
Till love dissolves mine inmost soul
    At its Redeemer's feet.

Be dead, my heart, to worldly charms;
    Be dead to ev'ry sin;
And tell the boldest foes without
    That Jesus reigns within.

My life with His connected stands,
    Nor asks a surer ground:
He keeps me in His gracious arms,
    Where heav'n itself is found.

Doddridge.

The Cross of Christ.

Aid me, O Christ, Thy cross to sing!
Its sov'reign virtues who can tell?
It takes a worm defiled with sin,
And makes him meet with God to dwell!

Brought near Thy cross, my soul shall melt,
And flow in streams of joy and grief;
For here my sins will all be felt,
And here's full prospect of relief.

The wrath of God by it's appeased;
His holy law is magnified;
Unbending justice is well pleased.
And heaven to earth again allied.

In virtue of its untold worth
What glories gild the heavenly plains!
What blessings have come down on earth!
Such as surpass e'en Gabriel's strains!

Around this cross the angels crowd,
Intent new wonders to explore;
And, raptured, all exclaim, " Of God
We never saw so much before !"

This cross a sinking world upholds;
Its power subdues death, hell, and sin;
High heaven's bright gates it wide unfolds,
And ushers happy millions in.

The triumphs of Thy cross push on,
O Christ, wherever sin is known!
Bid vice and misery begone,
And make the nations all Thy own.

The "travail of Thy soul" demand
The recompense of all Thy woe:
From every tribe, and tongue, and land,
Thy praise let all the people know!

Should e'er my love or zeal grow cold,
My caution fail, my faith abate,
Let me Thy cross, O Christ, behold:
That shall new life and love create!

Thy wondrous cross shall be my boast
While in this sinning world I stay;
And, when my voice in death is lost,
I'll sing it through eternal day!

T. Rippon.

The Call of the Heathen for Help.

From Greenland's icy mountains,
   From India's coral strand,
Where Afric's sunny fountains
   Roll down their golden sand;
From many an ancient river,
   From many a palmy plain,
They call us to deliver
   Their land from error's chain.

What though the spicy breezes
   Blow soft o'er Java's isle,
Though every prospect pleases,
   And only man is vile:
In vain with lavish kindness
   The gifts of God are strown;
The heathen, in his blindness,
   Bows down to wood and stone.

Can we, whose souls are lighted
   With wisdom from on high—
Can we to men benighted
   The lamp of life deny?
Salvation, O salvation!
   The joyful sound proclaim,
Till each remotest nation
   Has learn'd Messiah's name.

Waft, waft, ye winds, His story!
   And you, ye waters, roll,
Till, like a sea of glory,
   It spreads from pole to pole;
Till, o'er our ransom'd nature,
   The Lamb for sinners slain,
Redeemer, King, Creator,
   In bliss returns to reign.
               Heber.

Praise for Redeeming Love.

LET us *love*, and *sing*, and *wonder;*
   Let us *praise* the Saviour's name!
He has hush'd the law's loud thunder;
   He has quench'd Mount Sinai's flame:
He has wash'd us with His blood;
He has brought us nigh to God.

Let us *love* the Lord who bought us,
    Pitied us when enemies,
Call'd us by His grace, and taught us,
    Gave us ears, and gave us eyes:
He has wash'd us with His blood;
He presents our souls to God.

Let us *sing*, though fierce temptation
    Threaten hard to bear us down;
For the Lord, our strong salvation,
    Holds in view the conqueror's crown:
He who wash'd us with His blood
Soon will bring us home to God.

Let us *wonder:* grace and justice
    Join, and point to mercy's store;
When through grace in Christ our trust is,
    Justice smiles, and asks no more:
He who wash'd us with His blood
Has secured our way to God.

Let us *praise*, and join the chorus
    Of the saints enthroned on high.
Here they trusted Him before us:
    Now their praises fill the sky:
"Thou hast wash'd us with Thy blood;
Thou art worthy, Lamb of God!"

Hark! the name of Jesus sounded
  Loud from golden harps above!
Lord, we blush, and are confounded;
  Faint our praises, cold our love!
Wash our souls and songs with blood,
For by Thee we come to God.

Newton.

Christ's Atonement.

O Thou who didst Thy glory leave,
Apostate sinners to retrieve
  From nature's deadly fall,
If Thou hast bought me with a price,
My sins against me ne'er shall rise,
  For Thou hast borne them all.

And wast Thou punish'd in my stead?
Didst Thou without the city bleed
  To expiate my stain?
On earth my God vouchsafed to dwell,
And made of infinite avail
  The sufferings of the Man.

Behold Him for transgressors given!
Behold the incarnate King of heaven
  For us, His foes, expire!
Amazed, O earth, the tidings hear!
He bore, that we might never bear,
  His Father's righteous ire.

Ye saints, the Man of Sorrows bless;
The God for your unrighteousness
 Deputed to atone :
Praise, till, with all the ransom'd throng,
Ye sing the never-ending song,
 And see Him on His throne.

        Toplady.

Pleading the Atonement.

FATHER, God, who seest in me
Only sin and misery,
Turn to Thy anointed One,
Look on Thy belovèd Son ;
Him, and then the sinner, see ;
Look through Jesus' wounds on me.

Heavenly Father, Lord of all,
Hear, and show Thou hear'st my call !
Bow Thine ear, in mercy bow ;
Smile on me, a sinner, now ;
Now the stone to flesh convert,
Cast a look, and melt my heart.

Lord, I cannot let Thee go
Till a blessing Thou bestow.
Hear my Advocate Divine :
Lo ! to His, my suit I join.
Join'd with His, it cannot fail :
Let me now with Thee prevail !

Turn from me Thy glorious eyes,
To His bloody sacrifice,
To the full atonement made,
To the utmost ransom paid ;
And if mine, through Him, Thou art,
Speak Thy mercy to my heart.

Jesus, answer from above,
Is not all Thy nature love ?
Pity from Thine eye let fall ;
Bless me while on Thee I call.
Am I Thine, Thou Son of God ?
Take the purchase of Thy blood.

Father, see the Victim slain,
Offer'd up for guilty men ;
Hear His blood-prevailing cry ;
Let Thy bowels then reply !
Then through Him the sinner see ;
Then, in Jesus, look on me.

Anon.

The Disburdening.

Lay down thy burden here :
With such a weary load
Thou canst not climb yon hill,
Yon steep and rugged road.

'Tis rough, and wild, and high;
Thickets and rocks impede;
Scant resting-place between:
How canst thou upward speed?

Lay down thy burden here,
Poor, weary son of time;
So shall thy limbs be strong;
So shalt thou upward climb.

The sun is hot—no cloud
To shield thee from his ray;
It scorches up thy strength:
Stay now, poor climber, stay.

Thou breathest hard; the drops
Are on thy burning brow:
Try not another step;
Lay down thy burden now.

So shalt thou climb yon hill
Up to its steepest height,
Like eagle of the rock,
With easy, joyful flight;

So shalt thou bear the toils
Thy God appoints to thee;
So shalt thou serve thy God
In happy liberty.

Horatius Bonar.

Guide Me with Thy Counsel.

O GUIDE me ev'ry day;
  Ne'er let me go astray :
Shelter me ever near Thy side,
  With Thee let me abide.

To Thee I still will cling,
  And now my off'ring bring.
Accept it, Lord, and be my Friend
  Till time and being end.

Thy Spirit now impart
  To sanctify my heart,
And cleanse from sin's polluting stain,
  The source of care and pain.

For ever I will sing
  The praises of my King,
And louder, sweeter notes I'll raise
  In my declining days.

The wonders Thou hast wrought,
  The jewels Thou hast bought,
The burden of my song shall be,
  Till I Thy glory see.

In sweeter, higher lays,
  I'll shout a Saviour's praise,
For all the foretastes of His love,
  Emblems of joys above.

Amen, I now will say:
With me let blessings stay.
Thy presence now I will implore,
And grace for evermore.

Once more I ask and crave
Blessings beyond the grave.
O let me rise and dwell above
With Thee, the God of love!

Henry Jennings.

Loving-kindness of God.

Awake, my soul, in joyful lays,
And sing thy great Redeemer's praise:
He justly claims a song from me:
His loving-kindness, O how free!

He saw me ruin'd in the fall,
Yet loved me, notwithstanding all;
He saved me from my lost estate:
His loving-kindness, O how great!

Though numerous hosts of mighty foes,
Though earth and hell, my way oppose,
He safely leads my soul along:
His loving-kindness, O how strong!

When trouble, like a gloomy cloud,
Has gather'd thick and thunder'd loud,
He near my soul has always stood:
His loving-kindness, O how good!

Often I feel my sinful heart
Prone from my Jesus to depart;
But, though I have Him oft forgot,
His loving-kindness changes not.

Soon shall I pass the gloomy vale;
Soon all my mortal powers must fail:
O may my last expiring breath
His loving-kindness sing in death!

Then let me mount and soar away
To the bright world of endless day;
And sing, with rapture and surprise,
His loving-kindness in the skies.

Medley.

A Stranger Here.

I miss the dear paternal dwelling,
  Which mem'ry still undimm'd recalls,
A thousand early stories telling:
  I miss the venerable walls.

I miss the chamber of my childhood;
  I miss the shade of boyhood's tree,
The glen, the path, the cliff, the wild wood,
  The music of the well-known sea.

I miss the ivied haunt of moonlight;
  I miss the forest and the stream;
I miss the fragrant grove of noonlight;
  I miss our mountain's sunset gleam.

I miss the green slope, where, reposing,
   I mused upon the near and far,
Mark'd, one by one, each flow'ret closing,
   Watch'd, one by one, each opening star.

I miss the well-remember'd faces,
   The voices, forms of fresher days :
Time ploughs not up these deep-drawn traces ;
   These lines no ages can erase.

I miss them all; for, unforgetting,
   My spirit o'er the past still strays,
And, much its wasted years regretting,
   It treads again these shaded ways.

I mourn not that each early token
   Is now to me a faded flower,
Nor that the magic snare is broken
   That held me with its mystic power.

I murmur not that now a stranger
   I pass along the smiling earth :
I know the snare, I dread the danger,
   I hate the haunts, I shun the mirth.

My hopes are passing upwards, onward,
   And with my hopes my heart has gone :
My eye is turning skyward, sunward,
   Where glory brightens round yon throne.

My spirit seeks its dwelling yonder;
  And faith fore-dates the joyful day
When these old skies shall cease to sunder
  The one dear, loved-linked family.

Well-pleased I find years rolling o'er me,
  And hear, each day, time's measured tread:
Far fewer clouds now stretch before me;
  Behind me is the darkness spread.

And summer's suns are swiftly setting,
  And life moves downward in their train,
And autumn dews are fondly wetting
  The faded cheek of earth in vain.

December moons are coldly waning,
  And life with them is on the wane:
Storm-laden skies with sad complaining
  Bend blackly o'er the unsmiling main.

My future from my past unlinking,
  Each dying year untwines the spell.
The visible is swiftly sinking:
  Uprises the invisible.

To light, unchanging and eternal,
  From mists that sadden this bleak waste;
To scenes that smile for ever vernal,
  From winter's blackening leaf, I haste.

Earth, what a sorrow lies before thee !
  None like it in the shadowy past ;
The sharpest throe that ever tore thee,
  Even though the briefest and the last !

I see the fair moon veil her lustre ;
  I see the sackcloth of the sun ;
The shrouding of each starry cluster,
  The three-fold woe of earth begun.

I see the shadows of its sunset,
  And, wrapt in these, the Avenger's form ;
I see the Armageddon onset ;
  But I shall be above the storm.

There come the moaning and the sighing ;
  There comes the hot tear's heavy fall,
The thousand agonies of dying ;
  But I shall be beyond them all.

                                    Horatius Bonar.

Vanity.

Nay, 'tis not what we fancied it,
  This magic world of ours.
We thought its skies were only blue,
  Its fields all sun and flowers,

Its streams all summer-bright and glad,
  Its seas all smiles and calms,
Its paths from youth to age one long
  Green avenue of palms.

But clouds came up, with gloom and shade;
    Our sky was overcast;
The hot mist threw its blight around;
    Sunshine and flowers went past.

Hopes perish'd that had hung like wreaths
    Around youth's buoyant brow,
And joys, like wither'd autumn leaves,
    Dropp'd from the shaken bough.

Yet from these clouds comes forth the light,
    Light beaming from on high;
And from these faded flowers spring
    The flowers that cannot die.

Far fairer is the land we seek,
    A land without a tomb,
An everlasting resting-place,
    A sure and quiet home.

Far sunnier than the hills of time
    Are its eternal hills:
Far fresher than the rills of earth
    Are its eternal rills.

No blight can fall upon its flowers,
    No darkness fill its air:
It has a day for ever bright;
    For Christ, its Sun, is there.

O Sun of love and peace, arise ;
　Thy light upon us beam ;
For all this life is but a sleep,
　And all this world a dream.

Horatius Bonar.

Harmony of the Divine Perfections.

WHEN first the God of boundless grace
　Disclosed His kind design
To rescue our apostate race
　From misery, shame, and sin,

Quick through the realms of light and bliss
　The joyful tidings ran ;
Each heart exulted at the news
　That God would dwell with man.

Yet, midst their joys, they paused awhile,
　And ask'd, with strange surprise,
"But how can injured justice smile,
　Or look with pitying eyes ?

"Will the Almighty deign again
　To visit yonder world,
And hither bring rebellious men,
　Whence rebels once were hurl'd ?

"Their tears, and groans, and deep distress
　Aloud for mercy call ;
But, ah ! must truth and righteousness
　To mercy victims fall ?"

So spake the friends of God and man,
    Delighted, yet surprised,
Eager to know the wond'rous plan
    That Wisdom had devised.

The Son of God attentive heard,
    And quickly thus replied:
"In Me let mercy be revered,
    And justice satisfied.

"Behold! my vital blood I pour,
    A sacrifice to God:
Let angry justice now no more
    Demand the sinner's blood."

He spake, and heaven's high arches rung
    With universal praise:
He died! the friendly angels sung,
    Nor cease their rapturous lays.

                  Stennett.

The Divine Perfections Celebrated.

My grateful tongue, immortal King!
Thy mercy shall for ever sing;
My verse, to time's remotest day,
Thy truth in sacred notes display.

O say what strength shall vie with Thine?
What name among the seats Divine,
Of equal excellence possess'd,
Thy sov'reignty, great God, contest?

Thee, Lord, heaven's host their Leader own;
Thee might unbounded, Thee alone,
With endless majesty has crown'd;
And faith unsullied rests Thee round.

The heaven above and earth below,
Thee, Lord, their great possessor know :
By Thee this orb to being rose,
And all that nature's bounds inclose.

From Thee, amid the aërial space,
The north and south assume their place :
'Tis Thine the ocean's rage to guide,
And calm at will its swelling tide.

O blest the tribes whose willing ear
Awakes the festal shout to hear ;
Who thankful see, where'er they tread,
Thy favouring beams around them spread.

How shall they joy, from day to day,
Thy boundless mercy to display,
Thy righteousness, indulgent Lord,
With holy confidence record !

O wise in all Thy works ! Thy name
Let man's whole race aloud proclaim ;
And, grateful, through the length of days,
In ceaseless songs repeat Thy praise.

Merrick.

Christian Moderation.

Spring up, my soul, with ardent flight,
Nor let this earth delude thy sight
   With glitt'ring trifles gay and vain:
Wisdom Divine directs thy view
To objects ever grand and new,
   And faith displays the shining train.

Be dead, my hopes, to all below,
Nor let unbounded torrents flow
   When mourning o'er my wither'd joys.
So this deceitful world is known:
Possess'd, I call it not my own,
   Nor glory in its painted toys.

The empty pageant rolls along:
The giddy, inexperienced throng
   Pursue it with enchanted eyes.
It passeth with swift march away:
Still more and more its charms decay,
   Till the last gaudy colour dies.

My God, to Thee my soul shall turn,
For Thee my noblest passions burn,
   And drink in bliss from Thee alone:
I fix on that unchanging home
Where never-fading pleasures bloom,
   Fresh springing round Thy radiant throne.

Doddridge.

Lively Hope and Gracious Fear.

I was a grov'ling creature once,
  And basely cleaved to earth :
I wanted spirit to renounce
  The clod that gave me birth.

But God has breathed upon a worm,
  And sent me from above
Wings such as clothe an angel's form,
  The wings of joy and love.

With these to Pisgah's top I fly,
  And there delighted stand,
To view beneath a shining sky
  The spacious promised land.

The Lord of all the vast domain
  Has promised it to me ;
The length and breadth of all the plain,
  As far as faith can see.

How glorious is my privilege !
  To Thee for help I call.
I stand upon a mountain's edge :
  O save me, lest I fall !

Though much exalted in the Lord,
  My strength is not my own ;
Then let me tremble at His word,
  And none shall cast me down.

Cowper.

Providing Bags that Wax not Old, etc.

THESE mortal joys, how soon they fade!
   How swift they pass away!
The dying flow'r reclines its head,
   The beauty of a day!

The bags are rent, the treasures lost
   We fondly call'd our own:
Scarce could we the possession boast,
   And straight we found it gone.

But there are joys that cannot die,
   With God laid up in store;
Treasure beyond the changing sky
   Brighter than golden ore.

To that my rising heart aspires,
   Secure to find its rest,
And glories in such wide desires,
   Of all their wish possess'd.

The seeds which piety and love
   Have scatter'd here below
In the fair fertile fields above
   To ample harvests grow.

The mite my willing hands can give
   At Jesus' feet I lay:
Grace shall the humble gift receive,
   And Heav'n at large repay.

Doddridge.

Patience.

When languor and disease invade
 This trembling house of clay,
'Tis sweet to look beyond the cage,
 And long to fly away.

Sweet to look inward, and attend
 The whispers of His love;
Sweet to look upward to the place
 Where Jesus pleads above.

Sweet to look back, and see my name
 In life's fair book set down;
Sweet to look forward, and behold
 Eternal joys my own.

Sweet to reflect how grace Divine
 My sins on Jesus laid;
Sweet to remember that His blood
 My debt of sufferings paid.

Sweet on His righteousness to stand,
 Which saves from second death;
Sweet to experience, day by day,
 His Spirit's quickening breath.

Sweet on His faithfulness to rest,
 Whose love can never end;
Sweet on His covenant of grace
 For all things to depend.

Sweet in the confidence of faith
   To trust His firm decrees;
Sweet to lie passive in His hand,
   And know no will but His.

Sweet to rejoice in lively hope
   That, when my change shall come,
Angels will hover round my bed,
   And waft my spirit home.

There shall my disimprison'd soul
   Behold Him, and adore;
Be with His likeness satisfied,
   And grieve and sin no more;

Shall see Him wear that very flesh
   On which my guilt was lain;
His love intense, His merit fresh,
   As though but newly slain!

Soon, too, my slumbering dust shall hear
   The trumpet's quickening sound;
And, by my Saviour's power rebuilt,
   At His right hand be found.

These eyes shall see Him in that day,
   The God that died for me!
And all my rising bones shall say,
   Lord, who is like to Thee?

If such the views which grace unfolds,
    Weak as it is below,
What raptures must the Church above
    In Jesus' presence know!

If such the sweetness of the stream,
    What must the fountain be,
Where saints and angels draw their bliss
    Immediately from Thee!

O may the unction of these truths
    For ever with me stay,
Till, from her sinful cage dismiss'd,
    My spirit flies away!

                      Toplady.

Light's Teachings.

THE light is ever silent.
    It calls up voices over sea and earth,
    And fills the glowing air with harmonies—
    The lark's gay chant, the note of forest-dove,
    The lamb's quick bleat and the bee's earnest hum,
    The sea-bird's wingèd wail upon the wave.
    It wakes the voice of childhood, soft and clear;
    The city's noisy rush, the village stir,
    And the world's mighty murmur, that had sunk,
    For a short hour, to sleep upon the down
    That darkness spreads for wearied limbs and eyes.
    But still it sounds not, speaks not, whispers not!

Not one faint throb of its vast pulse is heard
By creature ear. How silent is the light!
Even when of old it waken'd Memnon's lyre,
It breathed no music of its own ; and still,
When at sweet sunrise, on its golden wings,
It brings the melodies of dawn to man,
It scatters them in silence o'er the earth.

The light is ever silent.
It sparkles on morn's million gems of dew,
It flings itself into the shower of noon,
It weaves its gold into the cloud of sunset,
Yet not a sound is heard. It dashes full
On yon broad rock, yet not an echo answers.
It lights in myriad drops upon the flower,
Yet not a blossom stirs. It does not move
The slightest film of floating gossamer,
Which the faint touch of insect's wing would shiver.

The light is ever silent,
Most silent of all heavenly silences ;
Not even the darkness stiller, nor so still.
Too swift for sound or speech, it rushes on
Right through the yielding skies, a massive flood
Of multitudinous beams ; an endless sea,
That flows, but ebbs not, breaking on the shore
Of this dark earth with never-ceasing wave ;
Yet, in its swiftest flow, or fullest spring-tide,
Giving less sound than does one falling blossom
Which the May breeze lays lightly on the sward.

Such let my life be here ;
    Not mark'd by noise, but by success alone ;
    Not known by bustle, but by useful deeds ;
    Quiet and gentle, clear and fair as light ;
    Yet full of its all-penetrating power,
    Its silent but resistless influence ;
    Making no needless sound, yet ever working,
    Hour after hour, upon a needy world !

Sunshine is ever calm.
    There are no tempests in yon sea of beams,
    That bright Pacific, on whose peaceful bosom
    All happy things come floating down to us.
    Light has no hurricane, no angry blast,
    No turbid torrent laying waste our plains.
    Morn after morn goes by, and the fresh light
    Pours in upon the darkness ; yet no storm
    Awakes, no eddy stirs the tranquil glow,
    No crested billow rises, and no foam,
    Drifting along, tells of some tumult past.

Sunshine is ever strong :
    No blast can break or bend one single ray.
    In seven-fold strength it faces wave and wind :
    Heedless of their opposing turbulence,
    It passes through them in its quiet power,
    Unruffled, and unbroken, and unbent.
    No might of armies and no rage of storms
    Can turn aside one sunbeam from its path,

Or bate its speed, or force it back again
To the far fountain-head from whence it came.

Sunshine is ever pure.
　No art of man can rob it of its beauty,
　Or stain its unpolluted heavenliness.
　It is the fairest, purest thing in nature,
　Fit type of that fair heaven where all is pure,
　And into which no evil thing can enter,
　Where darkness comes not, where no shadow falls,
　Where night and sin can have no dwelling-place.

Sunshine is ever joyous.
　Its birthplace is in yon bright orb which flings,
　O'er cliff and vale, its wealth of rosy smiles.
　Each sunbeam seems the very soul of joy :
　No sadness soils it ; scattering gladsomeness,
　Like a bright angel, onward still it moves.
　The very churchyard brightens as the ray
　Alights upon its tombstones, and the turf
　Seems strangely heaving to the radiant glow,
　As if fore-dating the expected sunrise,
　When, at the first gleam of the Morning Star,
　The faithful grave shall render up its treasure,
　And sunshine such as earth has never known
　Shall fill these skies with mirth, and smiles and beauty,
　Erasing each sad wrinkle from their brow,
　Which the long curse had deeply graven there.

Horatius Bonar.

Heavenward.

Come, let us join our friends above
    That have obtain'd the prize,
And on the eagle wings of love
    To joy celestial rise.
Let all the saints terrestrial sing
    With those to glory gone,
For all the servants of our King,
    In earth and heaven, are one.

One family, we dwell in Him,
    One Church, above, beneath,
Though now divided by the stream,
    The narrow stream of death.
One army of the living God,
    To His command we bow:
Part of His host hath cross'd the flood,
    And part is crossing now.

Ten thousand to their endless home
    This solemn moment fly;
And we are to the margin come,
    And we expect to die;
His militant embodied host,
    With wishful looks we stand,
And long to see that happy coast,
    And reach that heavenly land.

Our old companions in distress
　　We haste again to see,
And eager long for our release
　　And full felicity :
Even now by faith we join our hands
　　With those that went before,
And greet the blood-besprinkled bands
　　On the eternal shore.

Our spirits, too, shall quickly join,
　　Like theirs with glory crown'd,
And shout to see our Captain's sign,
　　To hear His trumpet sound.
O that we now might grasp our Guide!
　　O that the word were given !
Come, Lord of hosts, the waves divide,
　　And land us all in heaven !

Charles Wesley.

Birth of the Royal Prince.

Fair babe ! we hail thy royal birth,
Which scatters purest joy and mirth
Through every loyal heart on earth.
New joys date from thy natal day,
As every heart is heard to say,
A king and prince is born to-day.

The mother's pride, the father's joy,
His country's hope, the nation's boy,
May nought his peaceful reign destroy !
How gentle and how kind are they
Who watch and tend thee day by day,
Who ever care and for thee pray !
Gentle are those who hush to sleep
The little one whom angels keep,
And guard until the last long sleep.
How loving and how kind that one
Who fondly speaks the words " Now, come,
My little, precious, darling son !"
Heav'n bless the little royal son,
The Prince of Wales, his chosen one,
And say to them, at last, " Well done !"

Henry Jennings.

Contrition.

O Thou whose tender mercy hears
    Contrition's humble sigh,
Whose hand indulgent wipes the tears
    From sorrow's weeping eye,

See, low before Thy throne of grace,
    A wretched wanderer mourn :
Hast Thou not bid me seek Thy face ?
    Hast thou not said, Return ?

And shall my guilty fears prevail
   To drive me from Thy feet?
O let not this dear refuge fail,
   This only safe retreat!

Absent from Thee, my Guide, my Light,
   Without one cheering ray,
Through dangers, fears, and gloomy night,
   How desolate my way!

O shine on this benighted heart,
   With beams of mercy shine!
And let Thy healing voice impart
   A taste of joys Divine!

Thy presence only can bestow
   Delights which never cloy:
Be this my solace here below,
   And my eternal joy!

Steele.

Christ Crucified.

Now let us join with hearts and tongues,
And emulate the angels' songs:
Yea, sinners may address their King
In songs that angels cannot sing.

They praise the Lamb who once was slain :
But we can add a higher strain ;
Not only say, He suffer'd thus,
But that He suffer'd all for us.

P

Jesus, who pass'd the angels by,
Assumed our flesh to bleed and die ;
And still He makes it His abode ;
As man He fills the throne of God.

Our next of kin, our Brother, now,
Is He to whom the angels bow :
They join with us to praise His name,
But we the nearest interest claim.

But, ah ! how faint our praises rise !
Sure 'tis the wonder of the skies
That we, who share His richest love,
So cold and unconcern'd should prove.

O glorious hour ! it comes with speed,
When we, from sin and darkness freed,
Shall see the God who died for man,
And praise Him more than angels can.

Newton

A Deep and Broad River.

THERE is a river, deep and broad ;
    Its course no mortal knows ;
It fills with joy the church of God,
    And widens as it flows.

Clearer than crystal is the stream,
    And bright with endless day ;
The waves with every blessing teem,
    And life and health convey.

Where'er they flow contentions cease
 And love and meekness reign;
The Lord Himself commands the peace,
 And foes conspire in vain.

Along the shores angelic bands
 Watch every moving wave:
With holy joy their breast expands
 When men the waters crave.

Thither distressèd souls repair;
 The Lord invites them nigh;
They leave their cares and sorrows there,
 They drink, and never die.

Flow on, sweet stream, more largely flow;
 The earth with gladness fill;
Flow on, till all the Saviour know,
 And all obey His will.

Anon.

A Living Stream.

THERE is a stream which issues forth
 From God's eternal throne
And from the Lamb, a living stream,
 Clear as the crystal stone.

The stream doth water paradise;
 It makes the angels sing:
One cordial drop revives my heart;
 Hence all my joys do spring.

P 2

Such joys as are unspeakable,
  And full of glory too;
Such hidden manna, hidden pearls,
  As worldlings do not know.

Eye hath not seen, nor ear hath heard,
  From fancy 'tis conceal'd,
What Thou, Lord, hast laid up for Thine,
  And hast to me reveal'd.

I see Thy face, I hear Thy voice,
  I taste Thy sweetest love:
My soul doth leap; but O for wings,
  The wings of Noah's dove!

Then should I flee far hence away,
  Leaving this world of sin!
Then should my Lord put forth His hand,
  And kindly take me in!

Then should my soul with angels feast
  On joys that always last!
Blest be my God, the God of joy,
  Who gives me here a taste.

Mason.

A Blessing upon our Noble Queen.

God bless and save our noble Queen!
Till she shall join the Prince above,
In sweetest strains, in notes of love;
Till she shall join the angelic throng,

Where kings and princes sing the song,
Worthy the Lamb who died to save,
Who rose triumphant o'er the grave.
God bless and save our noble Queen!

God bless and save our noble Queen!
Till she shall meet and greet once more
The Prince on the eternal shore;
Where, clothed in pure and spotless white,
They'll dwell in light, unclouded light,
And tune their harps to nobler strains,
While crossing the celestial plains.
God bless and save our noble Queen!

God bless and save our noble Queen!
Till raptures fill the mansions bright,
Where God's the centre, God's the light:
Where hope and faith are lost in sight.
As long as life and time shall last,
O sanctify and bless the past,
And ward off every withering blast!
God bless and save our noble Queen!

God bless and save our noble Queen!
Help her to bear her heaviest care,
Till joys Divine she comes to share,
And feed on manna—princely fare:
Her aspirations raise above,
To Thee, her God, the God of love;
Send her the peaceful, heavenly Dove.
God bless and save our noble Queen!

God bless and save our noble Queen!
Be Thou to her a Husband, Friend,
While life shall last, till being end.
Thine ear to supplications lend:
In every trouble be her Friend.
O be to her supremely kind!
Revealing all Thy will and mind.
God bless and save our noble Queen!

God bless and save our noble Queen!
Help her to confide in Thee!
O may she all Thy glory see!
Still may she bear Thine image here,
And never, never yield to fear;
But, trusting in Thy power and love,
Wait till she join the Prince above.
God bless and save our noble Queen!

God bless and save our noble Queen!
Her offspring bless, and may they know
The source from whom all comforts flow—
The Saviour love, adore, and fear,
Who dries the mourner's falling tear,
Who folds the children to His breast,
And bids them seek the final rest.
God bless and save our noble Queen!

God bless and save our noble Queen!
Help all to join in songs of praise,
And nobler, sweeter anthems raise,
Until their spirits wing their flight

To realms of bliss and realms of light,
Where partings never shall be known,
But kindreds dwell before the throne,
God bless and save our noble Queen!

God bless and save our noble Queen!
Her offspring save, and guide their feet;
For joys celestial make them meet;
In kingly robes may they be dress'd,
And be for ever, ever blest:
Abundant grace to all impart,
That joy and love may fill each heart.
God bless and save our noble Queen!

God bless and save our noble Queen!
Her children, kingdom, subjects all,
To Thee will look, on Thee will call.
Our nation bless; all people save;
Make us victorious o'er the grave;
And brighter, brighter may we shine,
Till we behold Thee all Divine.
God bless and save our noble Queen!

Henry Jennings.

Que ma Volonté ne fasse pas, mais la Tienne.

Far in the windings of a vale,
    Close by a sheltering wood,
The sweet retreat of innocence,
    A pretty cottage stood.

There little Lizzie grew most fair,
    Beneath a mother's eye,
Who often breathed the fervent prayer,
    To meet beyond the sky.

The softest blush that nature spreads
    Gave colour to her cheek :
Such orient colour smiles through heaven,
    Where vernal mornings break.

The music of her voice we heard,
    As she gaily tripp'd along
Homeward, inspiring every heart
    With her sweet, cheerful song.

Soft as the dew from heav'n descends,
    Her gentle accents fell.
A friend beside her lowly bends,
    And whispers " All is well."

A mutual flame was quickly caught,
    Was quickly, too, reveal'd ;
For neither bosom lodged a wish
    That virtue keeps conceal'd.

Years of sunshine—years, years of bliss
    Were promised to this pair :
No cloud their sky could overcast,
    But all was bright and fair.

The voice, the eye, the hand, all spoke :
   Even Nature's song was love.
No joy like this is oft foretold,
   Till hearts shall meet above.

Alas! how soon the darkness comes !
   How soon all hopes are fled!
Prostrate the fair one lies, and then
   She's number'd with the dead.

Her cheek, where health with beauty glow'd,
   A deadly pale o'ercast :
So fades the fresh rose in its prime,
   Before the northern blast.

He came, her cold hand softly touch'd,
   And bathed with many a tear :
Fast falling o'er the primrose pale,
   So morning dews appear.

Lowly he bent to catch a sound :
   " She's gone," he once more cried—
" The fairest, sweetest child of earth !
   For her I would have died."

                 Henry Jennings.

Nil Desperandum.

Rejoice, though storms assail thee ;
   Rejoice, when skies are bright ;
Rejoice, though round thy pathway
   Is spread the gloom of night :

If the good hope be in thee
   That all at last is well,
Then let thy happy spirit
   With joyful feelings swell!

Look back on early childhood,
   And let thy soul rejoice!
Who then upheld thy goings,
   And tuned thy feeble voice?
Look back on youth's gay visions,
   When life one glory seem'd:
Who pour'd those rays of gladness
   Which on thy prospect beam'd?

Recall the hours of anguish,
   And let thy soul rejoice,
Though wave on wave of sorrow
   Rush on with fearful noise:
Was not the bow of promise
   Still seen amidst the gloom,
Shedding its hallow'd lustre
   E'en round the silent tomb?

Rejoice, rejoice for ever,
   Though earthly friends be gone!
For silently and swiftly
   The wheels of time roll on;
And still they bear thee forward
   Nearer that happy shore,
While the triumphant song is,
   Rejoice for evermore!

                                        Anon.

The Little Carol-singers.

SLOWLY they died away, those few faint embers,
Fading to ashes on the poor man's hearth.
'Twas one of those cold, snowy, bleak Decembers
That to the rich and happy call up mirth ;
But to the weary, desolate, care-worn poor
Hunger and pinching want come closer to the door.

The time of Jesus' birth was drawing nigh,
The time when angels visited the land,
When white-robed hosts, appearing in the sky,
Told of the blessings pour'd with lavish hand
From God Almighty's never-ending grace,
Shower'd on us below from His bright dwelling-place !

The poor man to his little children spoke,
And to his white-faced, weary, patient wife.
" Time was," he said, the silence as he broke,
" When glad and happy seem'd to me a life
When, poor though I might be, and cold and lone,
I should yet have some loved ones I might call my own ;

" And now I almost could have wish'd," he said,
" That you might leave this busy, care-worn land ;
That Jesus Christ would let you flee o'erhead,
Would take you with His ever-loving hand
To yon bright homestead in the starry sky,
Where you should never faint, nor, fainting, droop
    and die !"

But his wife spoke not—answer'd not a whit :
I think her spirit was so bow'd with grief,
She could not do aught besides quiet sit,
And bear the woes, and weary for relief.
And the young children, their bright eyes grown dim
Through many blinding tears, in wonder look'd at
    him.

Well, is the tale a sad one ?   I must mourn,
Declaring it is true : would it were not !
I would such ills were only fancy drawn,
Or e'en confined to one sin-stricken spot,
Instead of being spread so far and drear
That, wheresoe'er we turn, we find such pain and fear.

But would you cheer it ? would you have your care
Rescue your fellow-man from death, from sin ?
Would you, who have enough, and some to spare,
Open your hearts' closed doors, and take them in ?
What time is better than these Christmas days,
When angels came from heaven, their new-born Lord
    to praise ?

Then, at the last, one of the children cried,
A dark-eyed boy, who to his sister turn'd,
" I stood this morning a great house beside,
Brighter and brighter still the fire-light burn'd,
And rosy little children round it drew,
And O I wish'd so sadly I could feel it too !

"But come, dear Ellie, to them let us sing,
Sing those sweet carols that we know so well.
It may be they will help us; they may bring
A penny for us both : yes, who can tell?
Come, then, and we will sing of Jesus' birth,
Who, many long years past, at Christmas came on
    earth.

"It may be, too, that when *He* hears us sing
He will remember that we want for food.
He call'd the children to Him, welcoming,
And bless'd them once : I know that He is good.
Perhaps He may be glad our songs to hear,
And *He* may aid and bless us! come, then; do not
    fear."

And so they stepp'd forth on the untrodden snow,
And their young voices sounded sweet and glad.
O song, when is it that thou dost not so—
Gladdening the weary, comforting the sad,
And shedding peace and love on many a heart,
Light'ning its weight of sorrow, bidding grief depart?

They sang about the happy fatherland,
Where sin, and pain, and death for aye are o'er;
Where hunger, with its thin and bony hand,
Should threaten them with vengeance never more—
They sang, yet still no kindly voice did greet,
As the two children carolled down the snowy street.

But did they understand?   Not *all*, I know ;
And yet, in childhood's heart of tenderness,
The words that are not comprehended glow
In fairy colours fit to warm and bless.
Well I recall those fancies, sweet, yet wild ;
And it is not so long since *I* too was a child.

In that great house the boy had seen before
A young wife sat, and listen'd to the strain ;
And when the children's Christmas song was o'er
She waited till the sounds began again :
She leant her head, reflecting, on her hand,
And heard the wondrous tale of God's bright father-
　　land.

And then she rose, and to the window stepp'd,
And look'd on the soft snow, so pure and white—
All seem'd beneath its influence to have slept,
For all was still and hush'd—and then her sight
Fell on the carol-singers standing there,
While all around them blew the chill December air !

She had two darlings of her own to love,
And to her mother's heart the pity flew :
How would *she* feel, she thought, as, with quick move,
She to the door with hurried footsteps drew—
How would *she* feel if, in that bitter night,
Her precious babes stood barefoot on the snow so
　　white ?

She led them to the blazing, crackling fire,
And bid them warm them, while she brought them
    food ;
And the poor children's spirits mounted higher,
As they said, smiling, "Truly God is good ;
And Christ has not forgot that once He came,
A little child Himself, to save our souls from shame."

They went home happy ; and for many a day
The lady came to see and help them all ;
Until the father gladly oft would say,
"Now shame it was that so my faith should fall ;"
And the poor mother raised her head and smiled,
Nor trembled more to look upon each pale-faced
    child.

And think you that the lady felt it pain,
When her own babies climb'd upon her knee,
And she could tell them, o'er and o'er again,
Of those she saved from guilt and misery ?
Nay, rather, as she kiss'd each childish brow,
Joy, deepest, purest joy would fill her spirit now.

My tale is done. I pray you all who read
This ill-told story of a thing most true,
To hasten to some weary ones, who need
Some, at the least, of all that you can do :
Teach them that, in their grief, some do abide,
Who will not pass by, careless, on the other side.

And know that He who at this time came down
From His great heaven, to dwell on our poor earth,
Who left, for us, a kingdom and a crown,
That He might bring us mortals hope and mirth,
Sure *He* will see, though our faith is so dim,
And He will count it all as done indeed to Him.

Katie.

The Seen and the Unseen.—On the Great Exhibition, 1851.

HA! yon burst of crystal splendour,
   Sunlight, starlight, blent in one;
Starlight set in arctic azure,
   Sunlight from the burning zone!
Gold and silver, gems and marble,
   All creation's jewelry;
Earth's uncover'd waste of riches,
   Treasures of the ancient sea.
     Heir of glory,
   What is that to thee and me?

Iris and Aurora braided,
   How the woven colours shine!
Snow-gleams from an Alpine summit;
   Torch-light from a spar-roofed mine.

Like Arabia's matchless palace,
   Child of magic's strong decree;
One vast globe of living sapphire,
   Floor, walls, columns, canopy.
      Heir of glory,
What is that to thee and me?

Forms of beauty, shapes of wonder,
   Trophies of triumphant toil:
Never Athens, Rome, Palmyra,
   Gazed on such a costly spoil.
Dazzling the bewilder'd vision,
   More than princely pomp we see:
What the blaze of the Alhambra,
   Dome of emerald, to thee?
      Heir of glory,
What is that to thee and me?

Farthest cities pour their riches,
   Farthest empires muster here;
Art her jubilee proclaiming
   To the nations far and near.
From the crowd in wonder gazing
   Science claims the prostrate knee;
This her temple, diamond-blazing,
   Shrine of her idolatry.
      Heir of glory,
What is that to thee and me?

Q

Listen to her tale of wonder
   Of her plastic, potent spell :
'Tis a big and braggart story,
   Yet she tells it fair and well.
She the gifted, gay magician,
   Mistress of earth, air, and sea :
This majestic apparition,
   Offspring of her sorcery.
      Heir of glory,
   What is that to thee and me ?

What to that for which we're waiting
   Is this glittering earthly toy ?
Heavenly glory, holy splendour,
   Sum of grandeur, sum of joy :
Not the gems that time can tarnish,
   Not the hues that dim and die,
Not the glow that cheats the lover,
   Shaded with mortality.
      Heir of glory,
   That shall be for thee and me !

Not the light that leaves us darker ;
   Not the gleams that come and go ;
Not the mirth whose end is madness ;
   Not the joy whose fruit is woe ;
Not the notes that die at sunset ;
   Not the fashion of a day ;

But the everlasting beauty,
 And the endless melody.
  Heir of glory,
 That shall be for thee and me !

City of the pearl-bright portal ;
 City of the jasper wall ;
City of the golden pavement,
 Seat of endless festival ;
City of Jehovah, Salem,
 City of eternity,
To thy bridal-hall of gladness,
 From this prison, would I flee !
  Heir of glory,
 That shall be for thee and me !

Ah ! with such strange spells around me,
 Fairest of what earth calls fair,
How I need thy fairer image
 To undo the siren snare !
Lest the subtle serpent-tempter
 Lure me with his radiant lie ;
As if sin were sin no longer,
 Life were no more vanity.
  Heir of glory,
 What is that to thee and me ?

Yes, I need *thee*, heavenly city,
 My low spirit to upbear ;

Yes, I need thee, earth's enchantments
    So beguile me with their glare.
Let me see thee, then these fetters
    Break asunder, I am free ;
Then this pomp no longer chains me :
    Faith has won the victory.
        Heir of glory,
    That shall be for thee and me !

Soon, where earthly beauty blinds not,
    No excess of brilliance palls,
  Salem, city of the holy,
    We shall be within thy walls!
There, beside yon crystal river;
    There, beneath life's wondrous tree ;
There, with nought to cloud or sever,
    Ever with the Lamb to be :
        Heir of glory,
    That shall be for thee and me !

                 Horatius Bonar.

Prayer for Deliverance in the Judgment.

The last loud trumpet's wondrous sound
Shall wake the nations underground :
Where then, my God, shall I be found ?
When all shall stand before Thy throne ;
When Thou shalt make their sentence known,
And all Thy righteous judgment own !

Thou who for sinners felt such pain,
Whose precious blood the cross did stain,
Who did for us its curse sustain,
By all that man's redemption cost,
Let not my trembling soul be lost,
In storms of guilty terror toss'd.

Give me in that dread day a place
Among Thy chosen, faithful race,
The sons of God and heirs of grace.
Trembling, before Thy throne I bend :
My God, my Father, and my Friend,
Do not forsake me in the end.

Anon.

The Last Trumpet.

HARMONIOUS swells the joyful strain
To Him who died, and rose to reign ;
Jesus, who lives our cause to plead,
Whose voice shall call us from the dead.
   When the last trumpet sounds, the just
   Shall rise triumphant o'er the dust.

Though in the grave they silent lie,
They shall come forth, no more to die :
The body waits the final hour
That shows the great Redeemer's power.
   When the last trumpet sounds, the just
   Shall rise triumphant o'er the dust.

Now seated on His glorious throne,
He soon will come to claim His own ;
Soon shall they join His countless train,
Nor sin, nor death afflict again.
　When the last trumpet sounds, the just
　Shall rise triumphant o'er the dust.

Fly, time, away, with rapid wings,
And hasten on the hour that brings
The Saviour, clothed with power and grace,
And saints shall see Him face to face.
　When the last trumpet sounds, the just
　Shall rise triumphant o'er the dust.

Collyer.

The Books Opened.

METHINKS the last great day is come,
Methinks I hear the trumpet sound
That shakes the earth, rends every tomb,
And wakes the prisoners underground.

The mighty deep gives up her trust,
Awed by the Judge's high command :
Both small and great now quit their dust,
And round the dread tribunal stand.

Behold the awful books display'd,
Big with the important fates of men !
Each deed and word now public made,
As wrote by Heaven's unerring pen.

To every soul the books assign
The joyous or the dread reward.
Sinners in vain lament and pine:
No pleas the Judge will here regard.

Lord, when these awful leaves unfold,
May life's fair book my soul approve:
There may I read my name enroll'd,
And triumph in redeeming love.

Anon.

The Saint's Confidence in the Day of Judgment.

STAND the omnipotent decree;
   Jehovah's will be done!
Nature's end we wait to see,
   And hear her final groan:
Let this earth dissolve, and blend
In death the wicked and the just;
   Let those ponderous orbs descend,
     And grind us into dust.

Rests secure the righteous man,
   At his Redeemer's beck
Sure to emerge, and rise again,
   And mount above the wreck.
Lo! the heavenly spirit towers
Like flames o'er nature's funeral pyre,
   Triumphs in immortal powers,
     And claps his wings of fire!

Nothing hath the just to lose
    By worlds on worlds destroy'd :
Far beneath his feet, he views,
    With smiles, the flaming void ;
Sees this universe renew'd,
The grand millennial reign begun ;
    Shouts with all the sons of God,
    Around the eternal throne !

Resting in this glorious hope,
    To be at last restored,
Yield we now our bodies up
    To earthquake, plague, or sword ;
Listening for the call Divine,
The last trumpet of the seven :
    Soon our soul and dust shall join,
    And both fly up to heaven.

C. Wesley.

To Whom shall We Go?

Thou only Sovereign of my heart,
My Refuge, my almighty Friend—
And can my soul from Thee depart,
On whom alone my hopes depend ?

Whither, ah ! whither shall I go,
A wretched wanderer from my Lord ?
Can this dark world of sin and woe
One glimpse of happiness afford ?

Eternal life Thy words impart:
On these my fainting spirit lives;
Here sweeter comforts cheer my heart
Than all the round of nature gives.

Let earth's alluring joys combine;
While Thou art near, in vain they call:
One smile, one blissful smile of Thine,
My dearest Lord, outweighs them all.

Thy name my inmost powers adore:
Thou art my life, my joy, my care.
Depart from Thee! 'tis death—'tis more,
'Tis endless ruin, deep despair!

Low at Thy feet my soul would lie:
Here safety dwells, and peace Divine.
Still let me live beneath Thine eye;
For life, eternal life is Thine.

Steele.

God the Dwelling-place of His People.

Thou, Lord, through every changing scene,
Hast to Thy saints a refuge been,
Through every age, eternal God,
Their pleasing home, their safe abode.

In Thee our fathers sought their rest;
In Thee our fathers still are blest;
And, while the tomb confines their dust,
In Thee their souls abide and trust.

Lo, we are risen, a feeble race,
Awhile to fill our fathers' place :
Our helpless state with pity view,
And let us share their refuge too.

Through all the thorny paths we trace
In this uncertain wilderness,
When friends desert and foes invade,
Revive our heart and guard our head.

So, when this pilgrimage is o'er,
And we must dwell in flesh no more,
To Thee our separate souls shall come,
And find in Thee a surer home.

To Thee our infant race we leave :
Them may their fathers' God receive ;
That voices yet unform'd may raise
Succeeding hymns of humble praise.

Anon.

The Advantages of Knowledge.

Of all that live, and move, and breathe,
Man only rises o'er his birth ;
He looks above, around, beneath,
At once the heir of heav'n and earth :
Beyond the grave, with hope sublime,
Destined a nobler course to run,
In *his* career the end of time
Is but eternity begun !

What guides him in his high pursuit,
Opens, illumines, cheers his way,
Discerns th' immortal from the brute,
God's image from the mould of clay?
'Tis knowledge: knowledge to the soul
Is pow'r, and liberty, and peace,
And, while celestial ages roll,
The joys of knowledge shall increase.

Hail to the glorious plan! that spreads
This light with universal beams,
And through the human desert leads
Truth's living, pure, perpetual streams.
Behold a new creation rise,
New spirit breathed into a clod,
Whene'er the voice of wisdom cries,
"Man, know thyself, and fear thy God."

Montgomery.

"𝕺 𝕿hou that 𝕳earest 𝕻rayer!"

Thou, God! art a consuming fire,
    Yet mortals may find grace
From life's distractions to retire
    And meet Thee face to face.
Though "Holy, holy, holy Lord!"
    Seraph to seraph sings,
And angel hosts with one accord
    Worship with veiling wings;

Though earth Thy footstool, heav'n Thy throne,
    Thy way amidst the sea,
Thy path deep floods, Thy steps unknown,
    Thy counsels mystery;
Yet wilt Thou look on him who lies
    A suppliant at Thy feet,
And hearken to the feeblest cries
    That reach Thy mercy-seat.

Between the cherubim of old
    Thy glory was express'd;
But God in Christ we now behold,
    In flesh made manifest.
Through Him who all our sickness felt,
    Who all our sorrows bare;
Through Him in whom Thy fulness dwelt.
    We offer up our pray'r.

Touch'd with the feeling of our woes,
    Jesus, our High Priest, stands:
All our infirmities He knows;
    Our souls are in His hands:
He bears them up with strength Divine
    When at Thy feet we fall.
Lord, cause Thy face on us to shine;
    Hear us: on Thee we call.

Montgomery.

Life and Death—Time and Eternity.

O WHERE shall rest be found,
    Rest for the weary soul?
'Twere vain the ocean's depths to sound,
    Or pierce to either pole.
The world can never give
    The bliss for which we sigh :
'Tis not the whole of life to live,
    Nor all of death to die.

Beyond this vale of tears
    There is a life above,
Unmeasured by the flight of years,
    And all that life is love.
There is a death whose pang
    Outlasts the fleeting breath :
O what eternal horrors hang
    Around the second death !

Lord God of truth and grace !
    Teach us that death to shun,
Lest we be driven from Thy face,
    And evermore undone.
Here would we end our quest :
    Alone are found in Thee
The life of perfect love, the rest
    Of immortality.

                    Montgomery.

Saints in Heaven.

WHAT are these in bright array—
This innumerable throng,
Round the altar night and day,
Tuning their triumphant song?
" Worthy is the Lamb once slain,
Blessing, honour, glory, pow'r,
Wisdom, riches, to obtain;
New dominion, ev'ry hour."

These through fi'ry trials trod;
These from great affliction came :
Now before the throne of God,
Seal'd with His eternal name,
Clad in raiment pure and white,
Victor-palms in ev'ry hand,
Through their great Redeemer's might,
More than conquerors they stand.

Hunger, thirst, disease unknown,
On immortal fruits they feed;
Them the Lamb, amidst the throne,
Shall to living fountains lead;
Joy and gladness banish sighs,
Perfect love dispel their fears,
And for ever from their eyes
God shall wipe away all tears.

Montgomery.

Ask, and Ye shall Receive.

WHAT shall we ask of God in pray'r?
　　Whatever good we want;
Whatever man may seek to share,
　　Or God in wisdom grant:
Father of all our mercies! Thou
　　In whom we move and live,
Hear us, in heav'n, Thy dwelling, now,
　　And answer and forgive.

When, bound with sins and trespasses,
　　From wrath we fain would flee,
Lord, cancel our unrighteousness,
　　And set the captives free.
When, harass'd with ten thousand foes,
　　Our helplessness we feel,
O give the weary soul repose,
　　The wounded spirit heal!

When dire temptations gather round,
　　And threaten or allure,
By storm or calm in Thee be found
　　A refuge strong and sure.
When age advances may we grow
　　In faith, and hope, and love,
And walk in holiness below,
　　To holiness above.

When earthly joys and cares depart,
  Desire and envy cease,
Be Thou the portion of our heart:
  In Thee may we have peace.
When flames these elements destroy,
  And worlds in judgment stand,
May we lift up our heads with joy,
  And meet at Thy right hand.

Montgomery.

Religion.

Through shades and solitudes profound
The fainting trav'ller winds his way:
Bewild'ring meteors glare around,
And tempt his wand'ring feet astray.

Welcome, thrice welcome, to his eye,
The sudden moon's inspiring light,
When forth she sallies through the sky,
The guardian angel of the night.

Thus mortals blind and weak below
Pursue the phantom bliss in vain:
The world's a wilderness of woe,
And life a pilgrimage of pain,

Till mild religion from above
Descends, a sweet, engaging form,
The messenger of heav'nly love,
The bow of promise in a storm.

Then guilty passions wing their flight,
Sorrow, remorse, afflictions cease;
Religion's yoke is soft and light,
And all her paths are paths of peace.

Ambition, pride, revenge depart,
And folly flies her chast'ning rod;
She makes the humble, contrite heart
A temple of the living God.

Beyond the narrow vale of time,
Where bright, celestial ages roll,
To scenes eternal, scenes sublime,
She points the way, and leads the soul.

At her approach the grave appears
The gate of paradise restored;
Her voice the watching cherub hears,
And drops his double-flaming sword.

Baptized with her renewing fire,
May we the crown of glory gain;
Rise when the hosts of heav'n expire,
And reign with God—for ever reign.

Montgomery.

Thirsting for Divine Love.

O SEND me down a draught of love,
Or take me hence to drink above!
Here Marah's water fills my cup;
But there all griefs are swallow'd up.

R

Love here is scarce a faint desire;
But there the spark's a flaming fire:
Joys here are drops, that, passing, flee;
But there, an overflowing sea.

My faith, that sees so darkly here,
Will there resign to vision clear:
My hope, that's here a weary groan,
Will to fruition yield the throne.

Here fetters hamper freedom's wing;
But there the captive is a king;
And grace is like a buried seed;
But sinners there are saints indeed.

My portion here's a crumb at best;
But there, the Lamb's eternal feast:
My praise is now a smother'd fire;
But then I'll sing and never tire.

Now dusky shadows cloud my day;
But then the shades will flee away;
My Lord will break the dimming glass,
And show His glory face to face.

My numerous foes now beat me down;
But then I'll wear the victor's crown;
Yet all the revenues I'll bring
To Zion's everlasting King!

Ralph Erskine.

Come to Jesus Now.

COME, humbly bow before the Lord,
　His mercies now record:
Let ev'ry tongue His praises sing,
　For He is God and King.

Come boldly to the throne of grace;
　Come, see your Saviour's face,
And tell Him all your sorrows now,
　While you before Him bow.

Come in the exercise of faith;
　Come, for His mercy's great;
Confess your sins, and pardon crave:
　He'll freely bless and save.

Come, but depending on His love:
　For you He pleads above.
Come, for He calls: no longer stay;
　Obey His voice to-day.

Come, while He ever willing stands,
　With open heart and hands,
Ready to pardon and forgive,
　That you may with Him live.

Come, as a little feeble child,
　With a spirit meek and mild;
Come, trusting in your Father's love,
　Who lives and reigns above.

Come, listen to His gentle voice :
 He bids you now rejoice
In His salvation great and free,
 Which is for you and me.

Come in the morning of your days ;
 Come, sing your Saviour's praise ;
Then happiness will be your lot,
 And home a peaceful spot.

Come, morn and evening drawing near,
 For Jesus loves to hear :
Your faintest cry, your feeblest sigh,
 He hears beyond the sky.

Come while health and life are yours :
 Open wide are mercy's doors ;
Room there is for you, and all
 Who will for mercy call.

" Come, sinners, come," the Saviour cries,
 " As time so quickly flies ;
Come as you are, though poor and blind,
 And sight and riches find.

" Come, taste the sweetness of My love ;
 Come, join the saints above,
Who feast on princely manna there,
 Who know no strife, no care.

" Come, looking forward to the last,
   When the great solemn blast
Calls every nation from the tomb,
   And man receives his doom.

" Come now, and you shall ever share
   My kindness and My care;
The sting of death I'll take away,
   And give perpetual day.

" I'll raise you to My throne on high;
   I'll bless you when you die,
And carry you o'er death's cold shore,
   Where pains are felt no more."

Henry Jennings.

Christ's Presence Desired.

Jesus, I long to dwell
In joy ineffable,
Where saints and angels, ever bright,
Are clad in spotless white.

Jesus, I fain would rise
Beyond these lower skies,
Where every tear is wiped away,
And night is turn'd to day.

Jesus, I fain would fly
Upward to Thee on high,
Thy power and glory there to see,
Midst immortality.

Jesus, I long to go
Where saints for ever know
The riches of Thy heavenly grace,
The brightness of Thy face.

Jesus, I fain would soar
Where pains are felt no more:
My spirit longs to wing her flight
To Thee, where all is bright.

Jesus, I long to share,
And more Thine image bear,
Where all redeem'd at Thy right hand
In countless myriads stand.

Jesus, I long to see
That glorious liberty
Which all Thy chosen people share
Beyond this world of care.

Jesus, I fain would meet
The ransom'd at Thy feet,
And there join in the angelic choir,
And strike my sweetest lyre.

Jesus, I long to praise,
In sweeter, higher lays,
Thee, as the object of my love,
In princely courts above.

Jesus, I fain would stand
With all that happy band,
Who'll sing and praise for evermore
On the eternal shore.

Jesus, I long to find
Rest for the weary mind.
In Thee I trust, on Thee depend:
Let blessings now descend.

Jesus, I fain would tell
Thou hast done all things well:
With latest breath I'll praise Thee still,
And say "Be done Thy will."

Jesus, I long to greet
Friends round Thy mercy-seat,
And there to sing redeeming love
With all the hosts above.

Jesus, we'll then relate,
In that thrice happy state,
The wonders of Thy matchless love
In raising us above.

Jesus, to Thee I cry:
Receive me when I die;
O let a shining angel fly,
To bear my soul on high.

Henry Jennings.

A Prayer.

HEAR, gracious God! my humble moan;
  To Thee I breathe my sighs:
When will the mournful night be gone,
  And when my joys arise?

My God! O could I make the claim
  My Father and my Friend!
And call Thee mine by every name
  On which Thy saints depend!

By every name of power and love
  I would Thy grace entreat;
Nor should my humble hopes remove,
  Nor leave Thy sacred seat.

Yet, though my soul in darkness mourns,
  Thy word is all my stay;
Here I would rest till light returns:
  Thy presence makes my day.

Speak, Lord, and bid celestial peace
  Relieve my aching heart!
O smile, and bid my sorrows cease,
  And all the gloom depart!

Then shall my drooping spirit rise,
  And bless Thy healing rays,
And change these deep complaining sighs
  For songs of sacred praise!

Steele.

The Little Orphan Girl.

A PALE, thin, shivering child, an orphan girl, I met,
Whose clothes were ragged, and whose feet were very wet ;
For many were the rough winds and storms she had to brave,
Which sowed disease and brought her to an early grave.

The night was cloudy, dark, and drear ; the rain fell fast,
As I march'd on, with crowds, who also quickly pass'd :
The little sufferer sought, but could no shelter find,
Except in Him who is all-wise, all-good, and kind.

Though sunken eyes, though pallid, hollow cheeks cried help,
We onward went, and only thought and cared for self;
Our cloaks and coats we tightly drew ; thus warmly clad,
We heeded not the orphan girl who looked so sad.

We hurried to our happy homes, and there sat down,
Secure from raging storms and the world's chilling frown ;
The social smile we sought, and, sad to say, pass'd by
The suffering one, whose voice was heard by God on high.

To leave a child to brave the dangers of the night
Is most un-Christianlike—is very far from right :
Our duty is to rise and help the friendless poor,
To point to Him who gives, and gives for evermore.

Once more that night those gentle tones fell on my ear,
So very plaintive ! yet so very full and clear.
" I'll rise and find the child," I said, " this night ;
I'll wipe each falling tear, and make her burden light."

I sought and found the little friendless child of need :
I asked her where she lived—if she could read.
" I have no home, no friends," she said, with tearful eye :
" I'm left alone to beg, to starve, and then to die.

" My tale is true," she said, " but very hard to tell ;
Yet I have learnt to know that God does all things well ;
That if I look to Him, He will for me provide,
And be my Father, Friend, and my ne'er-failing Guide.

" My father, mother, brother, sisters, all are dead ;
Their happy, happy spirits are for ever fled
Beyond this lower world, to mansions in the skies :
I have a Father *there*, who never, never dies.

" There, in that land, where all is lovely, bright, and fair,
My Bible tells me all are happy, rich, and free from care ;
That hunger, want, can never, never there be known,
For all are fed by Him who calls the poor His own.

" Oft I am hungry here, but shall not hunger there.
Enough my Father has—abundance, and to spare :
My daily food and wants He can and will supply ;
He never leaves me, but He hears my feeblest cry.

" My Bible tells me I shall soon His glory share,
That I shall meet and sing with all my kindred there
The song of songs, and higher, louder, sweeter raise
My voice to Him whose love demands unceasing praise."

Henry Jennings.

Friendship.

FRIENDSHIP, how sweet to all, how dear!
It gently wipes the falling tear;
Its breath is sympathy and love,
Inspired by feelings from above.

It bids all fears and griefs depart;
It strives to heal the broken heart,
And with magic power to raise
The sweetest, purest song of praise.

Its voice is gentle, soft, and clear:
The weakest, meekest need not fear
To give this bright angelic guest
A place, a lodgment, in their breast.

Its gentle tones will hush to rest
The aching head and troubled breast!
It hears the orphan's bitter cry,
And points him to a home on high.

Friendship we will most highly prize,
Still more as every moment flies;
Nor shall it wane till we shall rise
Beyond, beyond these lower skies.

Henry Jennings.

Domine! Salve ne peream.

HELP and salvation, Lord, bestow,
 For these I greatly need:
None else these blessings can dispense;
 From Thee they must proceed.

Help me to look to Thee by faith,
   And all Thy glories see;
Save from an atheistic heart;
   Help me to trust in Thee.

Help me to cleave to Thee alone:
   Where else can sinners fly?
Save me from self-dependence, Lord:
   O hear my humble cry!

Help me to live upon Thy word,
   The Christian's daily food:
Save me from sin, that I may do
   Nothing but what is good.

Help me to grow in every grace,
   And holier, happier be:
Save me from sin in thought and deed,
   That I may live with Thee.

Help me to bear all trials here
   With meekness and with love:
Save from a proud, rebellious heart,
   That I may reign above.

Help me to feel that I am Thine,
   For ever Thine alone;
Save me by grace, and let me live,
   Hereafter, near Thy throne.

Henry Jennings.

Dulcis Luscinia. s. m.

HENRY JENNINGS,
August 12, 1863.

Vrai Toujours. c. m.

HENRY JENNINGS,
October 17, 1864.

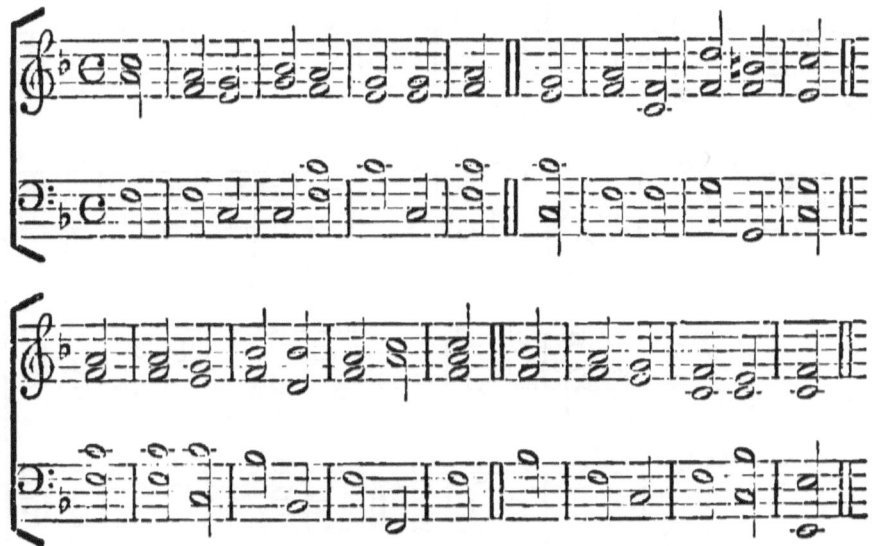

Tempori. L. M.   HENRY JENNINGS,
October 17, 1864.

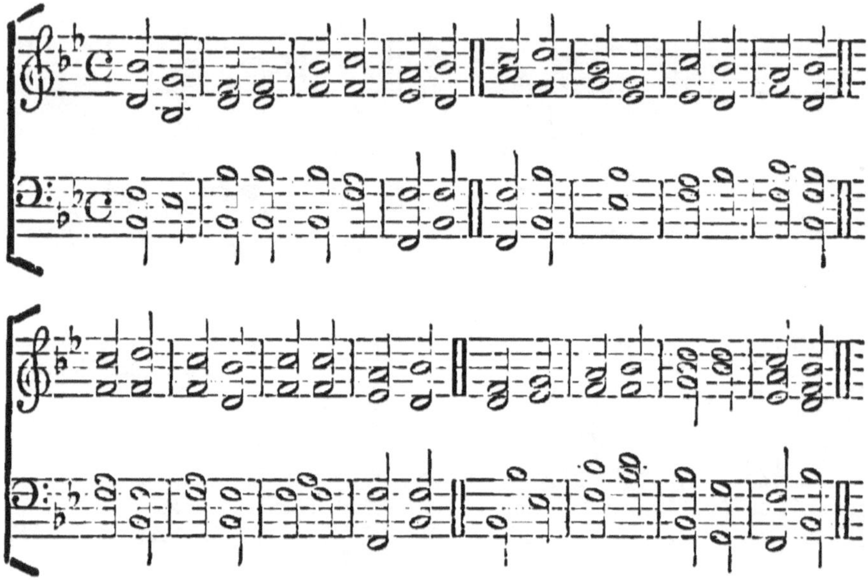

Psalle Entelligentia. C. M.   HENRY JENNINGS,
October 18, 1864.

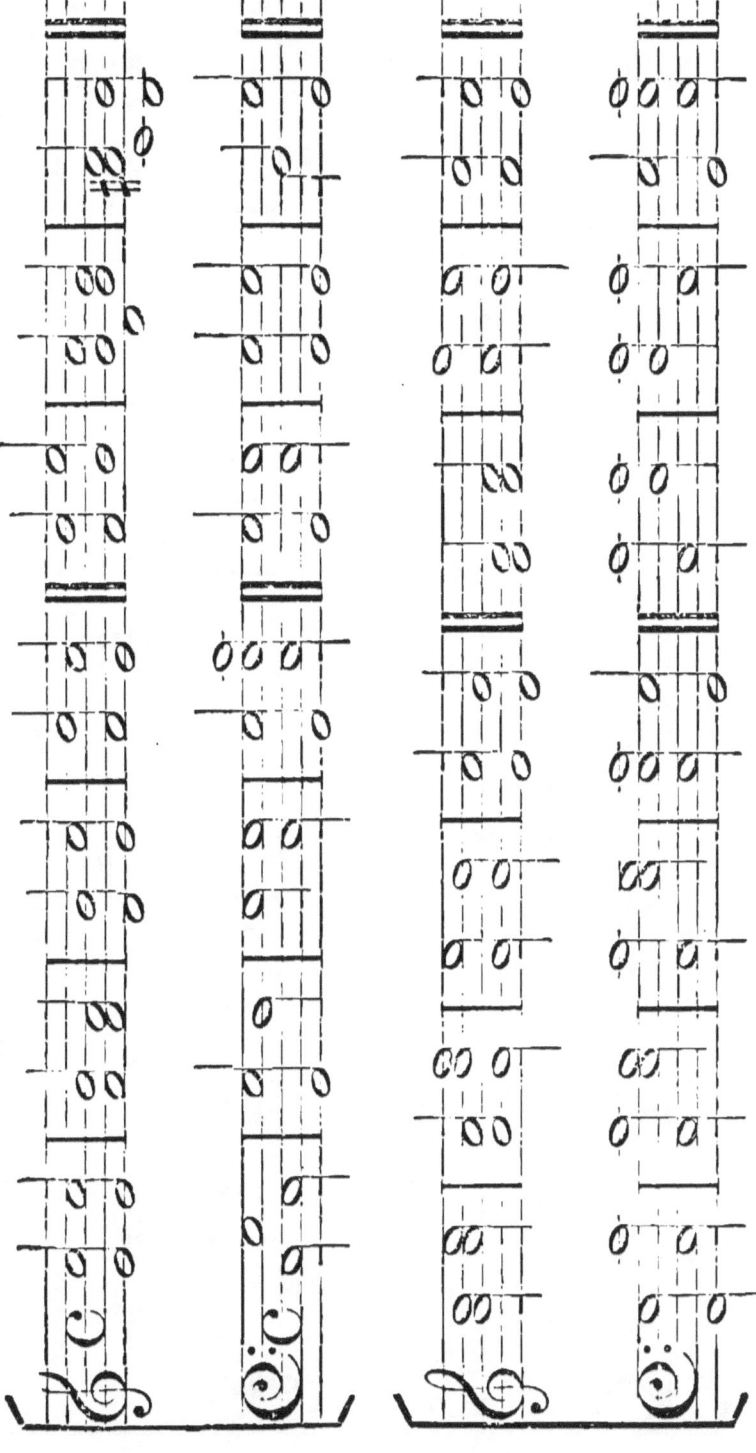

Chantez doucement et lentement.   C. M.

HENRY JENNINGS,
October 17, 1814.

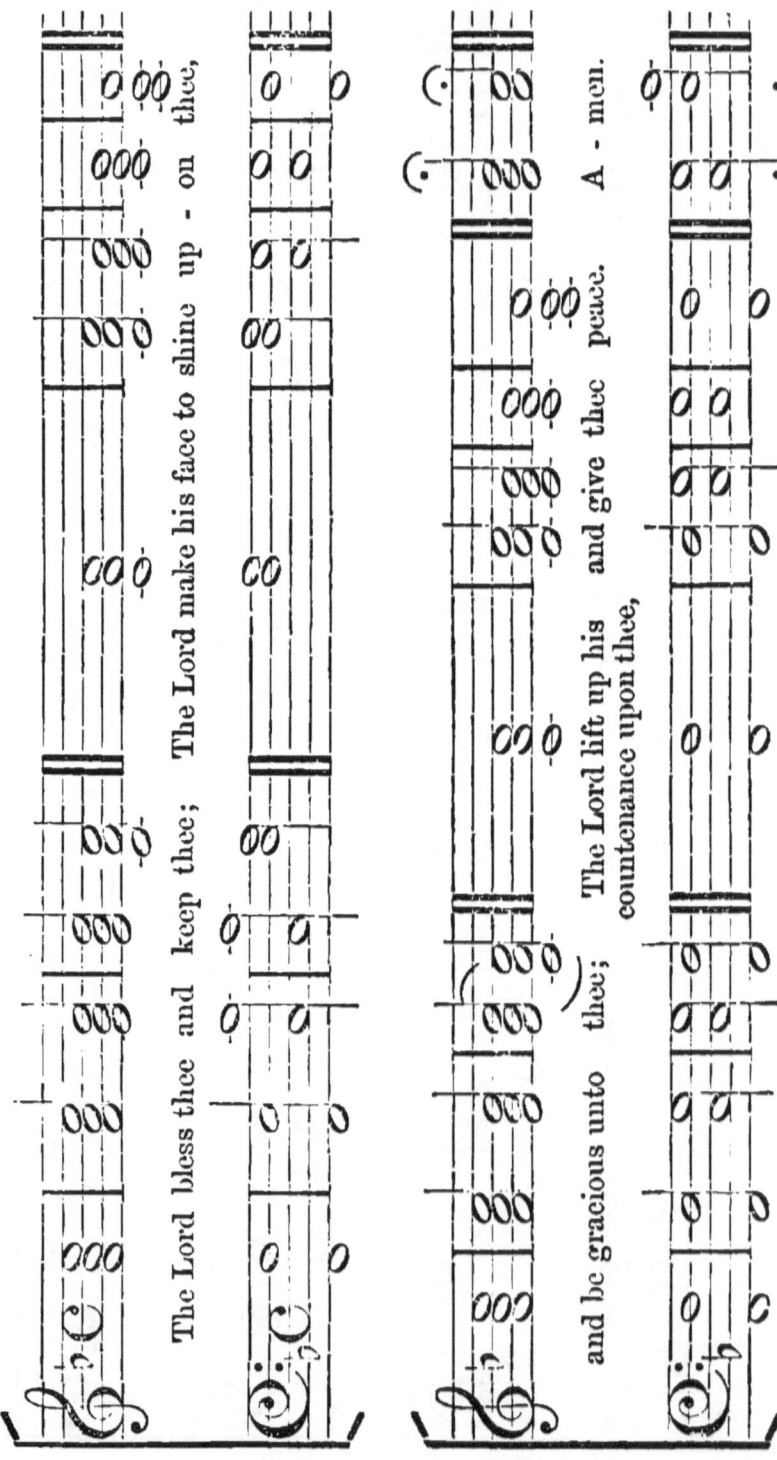

The Lord bless thee and keep thee.

HENRY JENNINGS.

The Lord bless thee and keep thee; The Lord make his face to shine up - on thee,

The Lord lift up his countenance upon thee, and be gracious unto thee; and give thee peace. A - men.

Index of First Lines.

Index of First Lines.

List of Authors.

WILLIAM STEVENS, PRINTER, 37, BELL YARD, TEMPLE BAR.